Classic
United States
Imperforate Stamps

By
Jon Rose

Published by *Linn's Stamp News*, the largest and most informative stamp newspaper in the world. *Linn's* is owned by Amos Press, 911 Vandemark Road, Sidney, Ohio 45365. Amos Press also publishes *Scott Stamp Monthly* and the Scott line of catalogs.

033071

Contents

Introduction

By Michael Laurence

The classic United States imperforate postage stamps, seven different designs introduced between 1847 and 1856, are among the most interesting stamps ever issued. They have been studied and written about extensively — in landmark reference works by such stamp giants as Stanley Ashbrook, Lester Brookman, Carroll Chase, Henry Hill, Mortimer Neinken and Elliott Perry. Regrettably, these works are long out of print. They command huge prices on the rare occasions when they become available. An unfortunate consequence is that details about the earliest United States stamps have been largely inaccessible to a generation of beginning collectors.

This book was created with those collectors in mind. It's the first of what we hope will become a series of popular handbooks, in this same format, treating a wide range of stamp and stamp-related subjects. We envision a series of well-illustrated monographs, conceived, created and priced to be within the grasp of the ordinary stamp collector.

Classic United States Imperforate Stamps does not attempt to duplicate the massively detailed studies of the previous generation. Instead, it presents high points from these works, updated to reflect new discoveries and insights that have surfaced since they were published, all amply supported by photos and illustrations. The basic objective is to give the casually interested collector a better understanding of these fascinating early stamps.

The author of this book, Jonathan W. Rose, is a professional journalist and a lifelong stamp collector. Rose's stamp and cover collecting interests range from

British North America to Zululand. He has exhibited a number of remarkable stamp and cover collections, winning major medals at national and international exhibitions.

For many years, Rose has written the Panorama USA column for *Stamp Collector*. He is editor of the prestigious quarterly journal of the U.S. 1869 Pictorial Research Associates. And he occasionally contributes to *Linn's Stamp News*. The book at hand had its roots in a series of articles Rose created for *Linn's* between 1983 and 1989.

Chapter 1

1847 5¢ Franklin

Date of Issue: July 1, 1847
Earliest Known Use: July 7, 1847
Scott Catalog Number: 1
Format: Two panes of 100
Designer: James Parsons Major
Engraver: Asher Brown Durant
Printer: Rawdon, Wright, Hatch & Edson of New York City
Quantity Printed (delivered to Post Office Department): 4,400,000
Quantity Issued: 3,700,000 (Brookman)

On July 1, 1847, the United States released its first general issue of stamps, the 5¢ value picturing Benjamin Franklin and the 10¢ black showing George Washington. This chapter deals with the 5¢ Franklin, a very popular stamp and, fortunately, a readily available one as well. Although the 5¢ stamp has been studied intensively for generations by a variety of experts, there are still questions to be answered and new finds to be made. The stamp has never been plated, and some authorities think that reconstructing the original plate layout is impossible, due to the lack of sufficient positioning characteristics, the result in part of rapid plate wear. Collectors continue to make new finds or rediscover valuable items. At the top of the rediscovery list is a missing cover postmarked San Francisco, used to New York City, bearing eight copies of the 5¢ 1847. Also sought is the 5¢ cover from St. Paul, Minnesota Territory.

The 5¢ Franklin was issued to prepay the half-ounce domestic letter rate for a single letter traveling less than

80RI (A)   90RI (B)

(C)   (D)

The four double transfer types of the U.S. 1847 5¢ Franklin: 80RI (A) features the double transfer of the top frameline; 90RI (B), double transfer of top and bottom framelines; (C), double transfer of bottom frameline and lower part of left frameline; and (D), double transfer of top, bottom and left framelines, also numerals.

300 miles. The 10¢ Washington paid the single letter rate for more than 300 miles. Double letters were charged double rates. The 5¢ Franklin was printed from a plate containing two panes of 100 stamps each. In 1850 the printers cleaned this plate, thus improving the printing impressions, which had become progressively poorer. This cleaning occurred between the third and fourth printing.

Some authorities attribute the deterioration in printing quality to the harmful effects of certain components of the ink. These were the earthen pigments — umber,

A $5 bank note of the New Orleans Canal & Banking Company. The engraved portrait of Benjamin Franklin at left is from the same master die used to create the 5¢ 1847 stamps.

ocher or sienna. The brown ink (pigment) was abrasive. The late Lester G. Brookman, philatelic author and stamp dealer, suggested that poor impressions resulted "as much from the results of indifferent printing as of plate wear." (See: *The United States Postage Stamps of the 19th Century*, Lester G. Brookman, 1966. H.L. Lindquist, Volume I, p.14.) Impressions of the 5¢ Franklin produced just prior to the plate cleaning and retouching in 1850 are badly worn and lack fine detail in the vignette and the ornate foliate frame.

After the plates were chemically cleaned and the shallow valleys restored to their original depths, the printings again produced sharp impressions. The 5¢ plates were made of steel. Printers made some 22,000 impressions from the 5¢ plate, producing about 4,400,000 copies. Only about 3,700,000 were sold.

No one knows precisely how many 5¢ 1847s still exist, but one authority, Creighton C. Hart, has estimated that as many as 10,000 covers may still survive bearing the 5¢ 1847 stamp. It would not be surprising to learn that at least 50,000 additional off-cover stamps exist — perhaps as many as 100,000. For the 1847 stamps, the ratio of on-cover survivors is quite high in comparison to

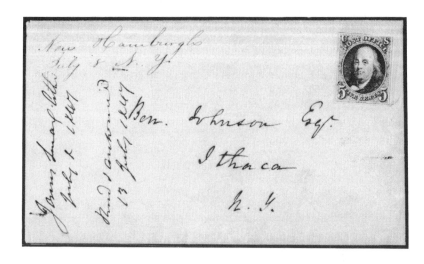

July 8, 1847 cover from New Hamburg to Ithaca, New York. A very early use of the 5¢ 1847 stamp, which had been released just a few days earlier.

subsequent stamp issues. In regard to 5¢ 1847 covers still extant, Hart has estimated that only about 10 percent or fewer bear stamps with four full margins. A similarly small percentage of off-cover stamps are of top quality.

The firm of Rawdon, Wright, Hatch & Edson of New York City, a company known for bank-note engraving, printed the 1847 stamps. Its initials (R.W.H & E) may be found in small letters at the bottom of the individual 5¢ and 10¢ 1847 stamps, just above the bottom frameline. The Franklin vignette on the 5¢ stamp is taken from a portrait by James B. Longacre. It was also the basis for a number of bank notes. The vignette was engraved by Asher B. Durant.

Although the 5¢ Franklins were issued on July 1, 1847, they were available on that date only in New York City. However, the earliest known 5¢ 1847 cover is July 7, from New York City to Poultney, Vermont. The cover is datelined July 6, and postmarked July 7 (New York City). A second 5¢ part-paid folded cover, an invoice dated July 7, 1847, is the earliest known use of the 5¢ stamp to a foreign destination. This cover was once in the Walter Hubbard collection. At the Siegel rarities sale in 1983, a 5¢ 1847 cover was sold bearing the manuscript dateline "July 8," showing 1847 docketing and containing a letter year-dated 1847. The 5¢ stamp was a deep orange brown, uncanceled. The envelope was sent from New

Hamburg, New York, to Ithaca, New York.

Boston received 1847 stamps on July 2, Philadelphia on July 7 and Washington July 9. In fact, the stamps were available that first month of July 1847 in only 11 cities, four of which received them on the last day of the month. The 1847 stamps were in use officially until July 1, 1851, when they were demonetized — declared invalid for postage. They could then be exchanged for cash until October 1, 1851. Since at that time postage still could be paid in cash, there are no examples of postmasters refusing to honor the 1847 stamps prior to October 1, 1851. The chief reason for the demonetization is that after the contract with Rawdon, Wright, Hatch & Edson expired, the dies and plates of the 5¢ and 10¢ stamps remained in the hands of the printers. For some reason, they insisted on this.

Despite the demonetization, many local postmasters disregarded the order or were indifferent to it. The 5¢ 1847s continued to be used as late as the 1870s in rare instances. A 5¢ 1847 stamp off cover is known canceled with a New York foreign mail strike, which could not have been used before 1870. The latest 5¢ 1847 cover is dated January 8, 1862 — a Confederate cover from Augusta, Georgia, to Eatonton, Georgia, with the U.S. stamp paying the 5¢ Confederate postage. A listing in the *American Philatelist* for March 1973, compiled by Hart, shows 43 late usage covers with 1847 stamps — i.e., covers used on or after July 1, 1851.

Plate varieties on the United States 5¢ 1847 stamp are not numerous, but several are distinctive. There are five major double transfers, four of which are well-described in the *Scott Specialized Catalogue of United States Stamps*. These are double transfers A and B, from positions 80R and 90R, respectively, and double transfers C and D, both much rarer because they come from the cleaned plate. Their positions on the plate are not known. Type D is so rare in fact that only one or two examples are known. And there are only about five copies of type C.

There is also the type E double transfer, or Mower shift, whose characteristics include double horizontal lines at the top of the "T" of "POST," and in the right arm of "U" of "US." This double transfer, or fresh entry, is also quite scarce. About eight or 10 copies are known.

The E double transfer was explained by Duane B. Garrett in *The Chronicle of the U.S. Classic Postal Issues*

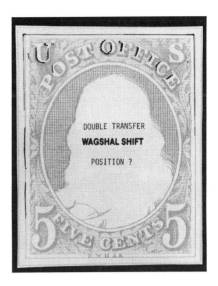

This diagram shows the principal points of doubling that exist on the three known copies of the Wagshal shift.

An example of the recently discovered Wagshal shift.

for November 1976.

More recently, philatelic researcher Jerome S. Wagshal, writing in *Opinions V*, a publication (1988) of the Philatelic Foundation, New York City, has laid claim to the discovery and elucidation of still another possible double transfer, as yet unplated. The doubling of the design occurs in both the left framelines and the letters "U" of "US," "O" of "POST" and all the letters of "OFFICE." Three copies of the new double transfer are now known. There does seem to be some question as to whether this new variety is related to the old "E" double transfer. More work remains to be done. Plating the 5¢ stamp is a Herculean task, which may never be effected in this century, if ever.

The dot in "S" (of "US") in the upper right corner appears on the stamps in the ninth vertical row of the left pane — 10 positions in all. This variety, an example of which is shown, carries a small price premium in Scott. Some copies of the 5¢ Franklin show what is called a preprinting paper fold. A section or corner of the stamp paper is doubled or folded over, and the design is then printed over this pleat. This is a natural occurrence and not a defect. Its price premium is marginal. Other copies exhibit marks resulting from scratches on the plate. One example shows a curl in the left numeral 5.

A specialist in the 5¢ 1847 can have quite a bit of fun in two areas: shades and cancellations. Shades run the gamut from the basic red brown through the dark true browns and orange brown to red orange and the true orange. The last two are extremely rare. The orange appeared in 1850. A very-fine used pair of the red orange

The "dot in S" variety appears on all stamps in the ninth vertical row of the left pane.

sold for $4,750 at the John Kaufmann sale in November 1977. A used single cataloged $550 at that time. On November 19, 1979, Danam Stamp Auctions sold a used 5¢ red-orange single for $8,000. Another delightful shade, one of four distinctive shades that appeared in 1847 (according to Dr. Carroll Chase's color study), is the black brown. A number of these seem to have originated in Philadelphia. Other shades include dark brown, grayish brown and olive brown. Chase's study ordered the various shades chronologically, which helps somewhat in dating covers lacking year dates.

In a series of three consecutive articles in the *Collectors Club Philatelist*, New York City (Volume 65, Numbers 3-5, 1986), Calvet Hahn re-examined shade varieties of the 5¢ 1847 Franklin. These studies were a long-overdue update of Dr. Carroll Chase's 1916 studies in the *Philatelic Gazette*.

Hahn concluded that there were five printings of the 5¢ Franklin, a conclusion reached by earlier researcher Creighton Hart. The third was from a worn plate; the fourth from a cleaned plate. Each printing had a group of ink shades and varying impressions. Ink manufacture and storage in the 1847-51 period was definitely not an exact science. Many shade varieties of the 5¢ stamp are available to collectors today resulting from this imprecision. Browns and, more rarely, oranges are the colors. All of the oranges and some of the browns are rare.

Cancellations are diverse on the 5¢ Franklin, as indicated in Scott. Colors include red, blue, black, magenta, orange, ultramarine, violet or purple (terms used interchangeably) and green. The last two are quite scarce. Chase also mentions a pink cancel from Chicago, which he called the rarest. Shown is a stamp canceled with a red grid marking with 13 thin bars. Another photo shows a copy with a rare red five-bar grid marking. An ink pen was frequently used to cancel the 1847 stamps. These pen-canceled copies are as valid as any with a stamped cancel, but collectors have tended to shun them. British stamps of the 19th century were used interchangeably for postage and revenue purposes, with revenue uses canceled in pen. These were less desired by collectors, creating a prejudice against manuscript cancels of all nations, even where the postal-revenue distinction never applied.

One expert on the issue, Duane B. Garrett of California, estimates that pen cancels occur on about 25 percent of the covers bearing stamps from the 1847 issue —

The paper on which this stamp was printed was pleated. After printing, the pleat was unfolded, causing the white stripe to appear down the design. Such freaks are not uncommon on classic United States stamps.

This 5¢ Franklin features a red grid marking with 13 thin bars.

This 5¢ 1847 shows a rare wide-spaced five-bar grid cancellation.

perhaps a higher percentage for 5¢ stamps on cover taken alone. The manuscript cancel was a perfectly legitimate use, spelled out in the postal regulations of the era.

Some of the distinctive postal markings found on 1847 covers include: "PAID," "FREE," railroad, U.S. Express Mail, "WAY," steamboat, steam, steamship, hotel, numeral, Canada and the Wheeling, Virginia, corner red grid control marking. These so-called precancels are not used to cancel the stamps and are found on rare covers whereon the stamp is usually canceled with a "PAID" or grid.

Specific rare and fancy cancel or postmark types include the Hudson 17-bar grid, generally in red; Binghamton, New York, herringbone (red, black — often counterfeited — and green); blue Trenton, New Jersey, star; Huntsville, Alabama, "PAID 5" in star; St. Johnsbury, Vermont, scarab; Troy & New York Steamboat in rectangle; and the green Princeton "5." There are many different "PAID" markings. A nice blue strike in a bold octagonal box is shown. It is from Philadelphia.

A steam or steamboat marking means that the cover was carried by an inland or coastal steamer with no government contract to carry the mails. These are service markings like "WAY." The handstamp "SHIP" indicates a contract vessel carried the cover. The Canada cancel usually means a specific type of ringed target, not to be confused with U.S. target markings, which happen to be scarce on 1847 stamps. The U.S. varieties are known used at Greenwich, New York, and Hanover, New Hampshire. The hotel marking is generally not struck upon the stamp, if ever, but is a private handstamp marking appearing elsewhere on the cover. It is very rare.

U.S. Express Mail postmarks are not rare and do not indicate extra fast service. In early stamp days, U.S. Mail route agents on the New York-Boston and New York-Albany (not after 1847) train runs used these postmarks.

The cream of the off-cover 5¢ 1847 items are those larger pieces, strips and blocks, unused and used, that grace important collections. Some of these have been consigned to museums. Among the more notable 5¢ 1847 multiples are the following:

(1) The square block of 16 (four by four), unused, original gum, the largest unused piece known, currently in the Ryohei Ishikawa collection, formerly in the Lord Crawford, Senator Ackerman and Philip Ward holdings.

(2) An irregular unused block of eight (two by three

Many different types of "PAID" markings exist on the 5¢ 1847 stamps. Shown here is a blue PAID in an octagonal box.

by two, originally three by three) from the Hirzel collection, now in the Swiss PTT Museum in Bern.

(3) A horizontal mint strip of eight, orange brown, last reported in the Ishikawa collection.

(4) An unused block of six (three by two), shown in the Brookman book, ex-Ward.

(5) Approximately eight additional unused blocks of four in varying conditions.

(6) A used block of 12, six by two, from the 1941 New York City find. The block — with eight stamps cut or gouged — was purchased by Norman Serphos of Scott Stamp & Coin Company.

(7) A used irregular block of 11 formerly in the Hawkins collection. (This may be the same block — with position 12 added in the four-by-three block — that is illustrated in Brookman, described as "badly soiled" and probably unused).

The largest known block of the 5¢ 1847 stamp, now in the matchless Ishikawa collection.

(8) A horizontal strip of 10, on cover, ex-Ackerman and Frank R. Sweet, now in the Ishikawa collection, paying the five times 10¢ rate from Washington, D.C., to Waukegan, Illinois. Used in 1851, it is the largest 5¢ 1847 multiple known on cover.

(9) A used block of eight, four by two, in the Hirzel collection in Bern.

(10) A used vertical block of eight, ex-Sir Nicholas Waterhouse, sold to Philip Ward in 1924 for $3,800; then in turn to Sinkler, Duckwall and Sweet.

(11) A horizontal strip of six on piece in the Hirzel collection in Bern.

(12) Two used blocks of four, one in light brown, the other of true brown, both in the Hirzel collection in Bern.

(13) A bank notice cover franked with a block of four, from Fredonia, New York, to Albany, New York, tied by orange grid, formerly in the Edward S. Knapp collection, now in the Ishikawa collection.

(14) Perhaps a few additional used blocks of four in varying conditions. Used blocks are scarcer than unused.

Specialists have intensively studied the on-cover uses of the first general issue United States stamp. As many as 10,000 covers survive showing one or more copies of the 5¢ 1847 Franklin stamp. Of these, there are perhaps 250 to 275 or so 5¢ 1847 covers used to foreign destinations. About 140 are known used to Europe, 85 to 90 to Canada and another 20 or so to Maritime provinces. Shown is a 5¢ 1847 stamp on a folded cover posted at Troy, New York, on October 29, 1849, addressed to "Staubridge, Canada East." The 5¢ stamp paid postage to the border. The manuscript "4 1/2" represents 4 1/2 pence Canadian postage due from the recipient. There are an additional seven or so 5¢ 1847 covers to such

A 5¢ 1847 stamp used in 1849 on a cover from Troy, New York, to Canada.

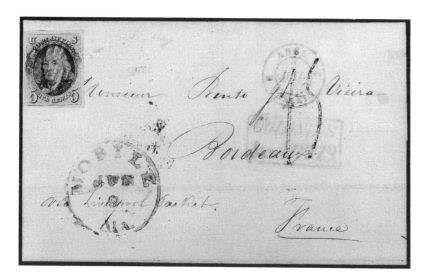

The U.S. 5¢ 1847 stamp on cover
from Mobile, Alabama, to France.

exotic destinations as Havana, China (Canton) and Santiago, Chile.

By early 1980 the listing of 5¢ 1847 covers compiled by Creighton Hart and Susan McDonald totaled almost 7,000. A May 1982 listing of 1847 covers to Europe, both 5¢ and 10¢, showed 55 to France, 72-plus to Great Britain, 27-plus to Germany, 14-plus to Holland, six to Belgium, three to Switzerland, and one each to Norway, Sweden and Gibraltar. The photo on this page shows a 5¢ 1847 stamp on a cover from Mobile to France. The squiggly black "15" represents 15 decimes postage collected from the recipient. In addition, there are a few uses from foreign countries, chiefly from Canada to the United States, as well as four 5¢ 1847 covers originating in Peru, going to Mexico via Panama.

There are more 10¢ 1847 covers than 5¢ 1847 covers used from Canada to the United States. A total of 65 genuine and bogus 1847 covers was noted by Hart and McDonald in *Chronicle 98* (May 1978). There are a few covers displaying the 3¢ Canada Beaver (Scott 1) and the 5¢ 1847 used together. They were legally used on the same cover only during the short period between April 6 and July 1, 1851. (A few 1847 stamps are known in mixed usage after the July 1, 1851, demonetization.)

The crown jewel of the Canada-U.S. 1847 covers is the cover that bears a strip of five 5¢ 1847s and a 3-penny Beaver, sent in May 1851, from Canada to London, via New York City. The Canadian stamp paid the rate to the border and the 25¢ in U.S. stamps overpaid by 1¢ the 24¢ rate from the United States to England, with the United States getting 3¢ and England 21¢.

Domestic usages of the 5¢ 1847 have been reported since the 1960s by Creighton Hart in various issues of the *Chronicle*. Some 5¢ domestic-origin covers are quite scarce; for example, territorials, and covers from Texas, Wisconsin and California. On the other hand, 5¢ 1847 covers from such cities as New York, Philadelphia, Boston and Baltimore are relatively common.

Two special groups of 5¢ 1847 covers deserve mention. These are the valentines and those covers where the 5¢ 1847 is used with a private local stamp, which pays the local delivery charge. There are some beautiful 5¢ 1847 valentine covers, ornate, embossed, lacy, in gold or color. These always bring a premium price at auction, although the stamps found on them are not always choice.

As for locals with our first stamp, perhaps the best known use is with the Blood's local of Philadelphia. Carrier stamps are also known with 1847 adhesives. These include several Philadelphia carriers, such as Scott 7LB1-5 and the "U.S. Mail" carriers (6LB9-11), issued by the postmaster at New York City in 1849-50. Carrier stamps usually paid the postage between post offices in one locality, or the charge for local delivery. Locals were issued by private firms that delivered letters to post offices (say to the Philadelphia Post Office, for carriage to a destination outside the city by U.S. mail) or carried mail from one point to another within the same city, bypassing the official mailstream.

Another very desirable use is that showing 5¢ and 10¢ 1847 stamps together on one cover. Perhaps 10 to 20 such covers or part covers are known. Two are in the Ishikawa collection, one with a 5¢ and a 10¢ used from

Five 5¢ 1847s, along with a 3-penny Canada Beaver, on a mixed-franking cover from Canada to London. This cover is currently in the collection of Ryohei Ishikawa.

Buffalo to Lockport, New York; the other showing a single 5¢ and two 10¢ stamps paying 25¢ of the 30¢ rate on a heavy 1851 letter from Rouse's Point to Plattsburgh, New York. Two similar 25¢ combination usages are illustrated in Brookman, Volume I, page 33. The one used to Nova Scotia is suspect; the two 10¢ stamps do not belong, according to Susan McDonald, editor of the prestigious *The Chronicle of the U.S. Classic Postal Issues.* (See *Chronicle* 78, p. 81.) There are also a few foreign destination 1847 combination covers, most rare. One of these, a cover to Belgium bearing 35¢ in postage, is shown here.

Finally, specialists should not neglect 5¢ 1847 proofs and essays, and the proofs overprinted "SPECIMEN." The 1847 regular issue was not overprinted "SPECIMEN." However, plate proofs of each value were. There was only one sheet of 200 copies of the orange brown and black of the 5¢ and the 10¢ overprinted diagonally "SPECIMEN." These, obviously, are rare. Unfortunately, available information on proofs and essays is dated. More current research is needed. Much of our information today was compiled by that great student Clarence Brazer 50 or so years ago.

Proof copies of the 5¢ 1847 may be divided into die and plate proofs in red brown on various papers, and trial color die proofs (large and small) in a rainbow of shades on various papers. The normal-color 5¢ Franklins include both large and small die proofs, the former being rarer. Large die proofs are found in red brown on a variety of papers: India, white bond, colored bond, white laid, bluish laid, yellowish wove, bluish wove, white wove and glazed paper.

Trial color proofs of the 5¢ 1847 include some 18

A single 5¢ 1847 stamp along with three 10¢ 1847s on a cover from the United States to Belgium. Covers showing both 1847 stamps are rare.

A large die trial color proof of the 5¢ 1847 stamp with cross-hatching lines.

shades printed on various papers (India, wove, glazed card, etc.) and issued more or less between 1858 and 1900. It is believed by some that these trial color proofs were made from a new die, fashioned in 1858 from the original transfer roll. The trial color die proofs, untrimmed, measure from about 35 millimeters by 42 millimeters to 50 millimeters by 70 millimeters. Many show cross-hatching lines surrounding the image area. These were engraved there to "prevent slippage," according to Hart. Some proofs don't show cross-hatching because the die was matted to eliminate it.

One should remember that the firm of Rawdon, Wright, Hatch & Edson, printer of the 1847 stamps, was absorbed on May 1, 1858, by the American Bank Note Company. American Bank Note was the printer of the die and trial color proofs, according to Brazer.

Only one plate proof sheet of 200 positions was made of the 5¢ from the original plate. These show no diagonal dash in the upper left frameline opposite the "U," (except for position 1), whereas the die proofs show this dashed line. The plate proof also has a position dot in the central leaf of the left trileaf ornament, Brazer noted.

Original essays of the 5¢ and 10¢ are rare and esoteric. Brazer had a set of original card essays (letter labels engraved, corner letters drawn in ink, frame wash and pencil), unique, supposedly done by James P. Major, head engraver of Rawdon, Wright, Hatch & Edson. A few die essays, showing either vignette or frame, are known printed on card as well as India paper. They too are rare.

Chapter 2

1847 10¢ Washington

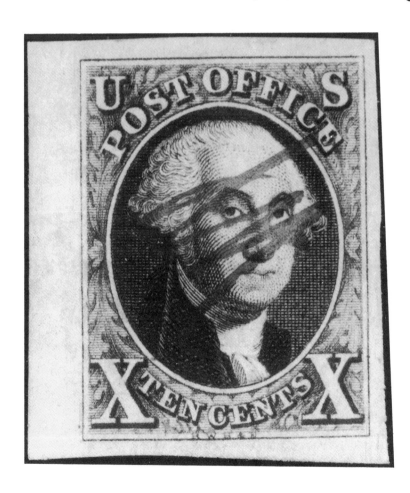

Date of Issue: July 1, 1847
Earliest Known Use: July 2, 1847
Scott Catalog Number: 2
Format: Two panes of 100
Designer: James Parsons Major
Engraver: Asher Brown Durant
Printer: Rawdon, Wright, Hatch & Edson, New York City
Quantity Printed (delivered to Post Office Department): 1,050,000
Quantity Issued: 891,000 (Brookman)

The United States 10¢ 1847 stamp, picturing George Washington after a painting by Gilbert Stuart, is a stamp to start the heart pounding. It has universal appeal for collectors of the classics. Like the 5¢ 1847 Franklin, the 10¢ black Washington is readily available at auction and elsewhere. Still, even in today's depressed stamp market, a very-fine used copy will bring more than $1,000. Extra-fine used copies can bring catalog or more, and unusual covers with singles or multiples sell for more that $2,000. This is not a modern phenomenon, as this quotation from a 1919 stamp journal indicates:

"Specializing in the 10¢ black U.S. stamp of 1847 is limited because of the decided scarcity of the stamp in fine condition. It catalogs this year at $8, but I have not noticed fine copies selling at auction for any such figure. The range seems to be from $12 to $15, with a few selling below $10." (*Early Bird,* June 21, 1919.)

I say all this because the collector who wishes to specialize in the 10¢ 1847 stamp must be patient as well as well-heeled.

The story of the 10¢ Washington has many twists and turns. There have been important finds of this stamp, and a score or more collections have boasted impressive arrays of the 10¢ 1847. Among the most important discoveries was the Ludlow-Beebee find of 10¢ covers, made in Philadelphia in 1923 by C.H. Bandholtz. This was a business correspondence that had been preserved. The find included 400 to 500 copies of the 10¢ 1847, including at least one strip of four and no fewer than nine strips of three.

The Ludlow-Beebee company had been located in New York City. A pair of 10¢ 1847s on cover from this correspondence is illustrated here. Many of the Ludlow-

A pair of 10¢ 1847 stamps on a cover from the famous Ludlow-Beebee find, a business correspondence discovered in 1923 that included more than 400 10¢ 1847 stamps.

Beebee (or Beebee Ludlow) covers bore express mail cancellations, and many of these wound up in the B.K. Miller collection, which was subsequently donated to the New York Public Library. The Miller collection at one time included 105 10¢ 1847 express mail covers.

In September 1927, the same C.H. Bandholtz discovered, this time in Portland, Maine, the two largest known pieces of the 10¢ 1847. These are an irregular block of 14 (positions 1-10, 11-14L) and a strip of 10, both originally used together on a parcel sent from Cleveland to Providence. These items were sold to George F. Tyler, then to Frank R. Sweet, of Attleboro, Massachusetts. Sweet purchased them for what was claimed at that time to be "the highest price yet paid for a U.S. item not even excluding the sheet of the 24¢ airmail inverts," according to the late Lester G. Brookman. H.R. Harmer, Inc. of New York City sold the Sweet collection of 10¢ 1847s in 1960. The two Bandholtz pieces combined realized $12,000 — most reasonable.

As recently as 1972, Harry Mark, a tax consultant, made a great 10¢ 1847 discovery in Indianapolis. Mark found buried in a law book a cover franked with a horizontal pair of the 10¢ 1847. The cover has a New York City postmark of July 2. The year date, 1847, is proven by the contents of the cover, which are intact and genuine. This represents a second day of usage of a 10¢ 1847, and is the earliest known use of either 1847 stamp, 5¢ or 10¢. The stamps are from position 61-62L. The pair paid most of the 30¢ postage due on this triple-rate legal cover, the rest being collected in cash at Indianapolis. The cover is addressed to the clerk of the Marion Circuit Court, Marion County, Indiana. It was illustrated and discussed in the August 1972 *American Philatelist.*

Prior to the discovery of the Indianapolis cover, the earliest known use of a 10¢ 1847 was on a July 9 cover from New York City to Galena, Illinois. The third earliest known is dated July 10 (1847) and was sent from New York City to Louisville, Kentucky.

Writing about the July 2 cover, Susan McDonald said (in the May 1972 *Chronicle*):

"Absolute proof that the (1847) stamps were sold at the New York City Post Office on July 1, 1847, may never be established, unless a July 1 cover or other documentation can be produced, but the preponderance of evidence supports this belief."

Most of the important pieces wind up in important collections, and there have been some impressive hold-

A caricature from the cover of *Pat Paragraphs*, the scholarly house organ of Elliott Perry, who plated the 10¢ 1847 stamp.

ings of the 10¢ 1847 amassed during the past 50 to 60 years. In any discussion of famous 1847 holdings, one would have to start with that of Senator Ernest R. Ackerman of New Jersey. The Ackerman collection contained about 1,200 copies of the 5¢ 1847 and 400 of the 10¢ stamp. It included major portions of the impressive A.K. McDaniel and Dr. Carroll Chase collections of the 10¢ 1847. When the Ackerman collection was dispersed by Elliott Perry, it comprised 14 volumes of 1847s, with an estimated retail value of more than $100,000 — in 1931.

Perhaps the most impressive item was the complete plating reconstruction of the two panes of 100 of the 10¢ 1847, all 200 positions properly "plated." This was largely the work of Elliott Perry himself, one of the monumental achievements of U.S. philatelic research. Shown is a caricature by Perry, taken from the cover of *Pat Paragraphs*, a house organ/research journal that Perry published for many years.

The story behind the plating of the 10¢ 1847s is worth telling. Perry had been helping build the Ackerman collection of 1847s, with the intention of showing part of it at the big International Philatelic Exhibition in London set for May 1923. Perry had to pare down and rearrange the 1847s to suit the exhibit. In December 1922, he sailed for England to make preliminary arrangements for the showing. On the leisurely transatlantic voyage, Perry occupied his time sorting and sifting the material. He had nurtured an idea that perhaps the 10¢ 1847s could be plated, and this was on his mind as he arranged the collection.

Among the material he discovered a 10¢ straddle pane copy (which had been in the McDaniel collection)

Horizontal strip of six 10¢ 1847 stamps on a cover from Philadelphia to Paris. This item was once described as ". . . the most important cover known to American philately ."

18

from position 1R, the first stamp in the right pane. This showed the complete between-panes gutter and a small part of the stamp from the adjoining position on the left pane (position 10L). This discovery helped convince Perry that the plating task was possible. He also was sure now that the 10¢ plate consisted of two panes of 100 positions each. (He knew of a horizontal strip of six of the 10¢, which eliminated the possibility of a five-by-ten stamp pane layout.)

Before reaching England, Perry had found 125 distinct varieties of the 10¢ stamp. By overlapping pairs and other multiple copies, he could assign about 50 stamps to definite plate positions. When he returned from England, Perry solicited the aid of other collectors. He was soon able to obtain enough copies of the 1847, especially multiples, to determine specific plate position characteristics for all 200 stamps on the plate. He was able to do this through study of framelines, guidelines and, especially, position dots.

In preparing the printing plate, these position dots helped the operator adjust the transfer roll to the correct position in transferring the stamp design into the plate. These tiny dots are usually located in the three-leaf ornament in the middle of the left side of the stamp. Perry observed that parts of the 10¢ stamp design had been recut before any stamps were printed from the plate, in order to strengthen the other framelines. On the die, the

The largest surviving mint multiple of the 10¢ 1847 stamp, a block of six now in the Ryohei Ishikawa collection.

framelines were thin, probably damaged in transferring.

Perry's 10¢ 1847 plating study was published in consecutive issues of *The Collectors Club Philatelist* during the years 1924-1926. Included were detailed illustrations of all 200 positions.

A second remarkable collection of the past was that of Henry C. Gibson. This Philadelphia businessman possessed a marvelous group of U.S. covers. His 1847s were second to none. Noteworthy was a cover with a horizontal strip of six 10¢ 1847 stamps, tied by bright red "5's" in circles. Mailed in September 1848, the cover went from Philadelphia to Paris, the recipient there being Richard Rush, U.S. minister to France.

Philip H. Ward Jr., who sold the Gibson collection in 1944, wrote of this cover: "We consider this the most important cover known to American philately." It sold then for $4,000. The cover is illustrated on page 18. In the same sale, the famous cover (shown on page 12) with a strip of five 5¢ 1847s and a 3-penny Canada Beaver on laid paper sold for even more, at $6,000. Another Gibson cover had a single 5¢ and a horizontal strip of three of the 10¢ 1847 to Belgium, used November 1848. Someone walked off with this for $700. Also in the sale were two 10¢ diagonal bisect covers (more about these later), as well as a Kennedy correspondence cover with a 10¢ 1847 used from Canada to New York City.

The U.S. cover collection of Emmerson C. Krug, sold in 1958 by Robert A. Siegel, contained a fine batch of 1847 items, including 24 5¢ and 10¢ covers used to foreign countries. There was a 10¢ 1847 cover used to Scotland and another to Germany. Krug's holdings also featured the cover with a 5¢ 1847 and two 10¢, used on

Eight 10¢ 1847s paying twice the 40¢ rate from New York to California in February 1850.

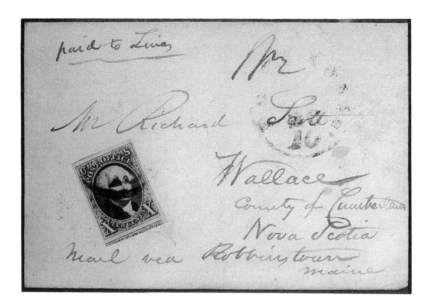

A four-margin 10¢ 1847 stamp on cover to Nova Scotia.

a legal size cover (5 due) from Rouse's Point, New York, to Plattsburgh, New York. This item, previously mentioned on page 12, is now in the international award-winning U.S. classic collection of Ryohei Ishikawa of Tokyo. Krug also had two covers with pairs of the 10¢, one a horizontal and the other a vertical pair, much scarcer.

In 1950, H.R. Harmer auctioned the William L. Moody collection. This included 114 lots of 1847s, featuring unused copies of the 5¢ (four different shades) and 10¢, a full sheet margin copy of the 5¢, a lower right 10¢ corner copy, four 10¢ bisect covers (including a right vertical half) and the unique 10¢ cover from Galveston, Texas, the stamp tied by the handstamp, "WAY 11 CENTS."

Sir Nicholas Waterhouse, an Englishman, had 67 lots of 1847 material when Harmers of London sold his collection in 1955. Included was an unused vertical strip of three of the 10¢, the upper pair being superb. Waterhouse also had one of the scarce 5¢ plus 10¢ 1847 combination covers.

Siegel's sale on October 31, 1957, comprised 312 lots of 1847 material, including more than 70 10¢ covers. Among these was the famous cover from Waukegan, Illinois, to Canandaigua, New York, bearing a superb horizontal strip of four 10¢ 1847s, tied by the distinct red six-bar Waukegan grids. This item is also now in the Ishikawa collection. The sale was also highlighted by 5¢ and 10¢

1847 covers used to England and four 5¢ covers to France.

Alfred H. Caspary's famous worldwide collection, sold about the same time by H.R. Harmer, had 171 lots of 1847 material. Ten-cent 1847 pieces included three unused pairs, one vertical; three used pairs; and a horizontal strip of five. Covers included one from Philadelphia to Pittsburgh with four singles; the Waukegan cover to Sprakers Basin, New York, strip of four; 10¢ used from Canada (Morgan correspondence); and four 10¢ bisect covers, three diagonal and one vertical.

The collection of Saul Newbury included many extremely choice U.S. classic stamps. Siegel sold the material during a series of auctions in 1961 and 1963. In the 204 lots of 1847 material was a combination 5¢ plus 10¢ cover with a Naugatuck R.R. cancel from Derby, Connecticut, to New York City (sold for $2,000) and beautiful matched sheet corner copies of both the 5¢ and 10¢, used, positions 100R and 91L, respectively.

Today, many of the famous 10¢ 1847 pieces and covers are in the collections of Ryohei Ishikawa of Tokyo; Leonard Kapiloff of Rockville, Maryland; and several collections in the Midwest, South and East, never publicly exhibited.

Ishikawa has the remarkable restored cover with nine copies of the 10¢ 1847 paying three times the 30¢ rate from Lima, Peru, to Tepic, Mexico, used July 13, 1850. This record cover (most 10¢ 1847s on one cover) was once in the "Via Panama" collection of Colonel James T. DeVoss. The cover sold in 1978 for $50,000. The largest unused multiple, a horizontal block of six (shown on page 19), ex-Ward, is also in the Ishikawa holding.

Leonard Kapiloff owns many wonderful 10¢ covers, including one to California with eight copies of the 10¢ (two times 40¢ rate) and another with four copies. California became a state on September 8, 1850. After the Treaty of Guadalupe-Hidalgo (proclaimed July 4, 1848), California had had first a military government and then local civil government. By the Act of Congress of August 14, 1848, 40¢ per half ounce was the declared rate on letters between California and the East Coast. (The letter rate within California was 12 1/2¢.) There are 12 recorded 1847 covers to California. All but three are 40¢ rate covers paid by four 10¢ stamps. One 10¢ 1847 cover is known to have originated in California paying the 40¢ rate eastward. This folded letter was sent from San Francisco in January 1851 to the New York firm of

Howland & Aspinwall. California received no 1847 stamps officially, so the stamps were either carried or mailed to California. The strip of four on the eastbound cover is canceled with red "PAID" strikes, one of which ties, and long diagonal manuscript pen marks.

The Kapiloff cover with eight 10¢ 1847s, shown on page 20, is franked with strips of five and three. It was sent February 7, 1850, from New York City to San Francisco. It is the only known usage of the double 40¢ rate from coast to coast during the 1847 period. Red "PAID" cancels tie the strips to the cover.

Virtually every great collection of the 10¢ 1847 has included impressive covers. But it wasn't until fairly recently that anyone made an attempt to list them all. *The Directory of 10¢ 1847 Covers* was compiled by Creighton C. Hart and Susan M. McDonald and published in 1970. In it are listed, more or less in chronological order, more than 1,800 covers. Since then the list has been expanded (but not yet published) to about 2,300-plus covers of the 2,500 10¢ 1847 covers that Hart estimates still exist. Between 5 and 10 percent of those listed are designated as fakes. Originally released for a $10 donation, the *Directory* now sells at auction for at least $150.

A totl of 891,000 copies of the 10¢ 1847 stamp were issued to postmasters. Bear in mind that some experts say that only about one letter in 100 sent during 1847-51 bore stamps. Of the 2,000 or so genuine 10¢ 1847 covers known to exist, about 200 are used to Canada. Also, a majority of the 38 additional 1847-stamp covers known used to the Maritime Provinces are 10¢ 1847s, rather than 5¢ 1847s.

There are five genuine 10¢ covers known used to

This may be the only cover in existence showing both the over and under 300-hundred-mile single rate prepaid by stamps of the correct denomination. The cover was mailed from Buffalo to Albany, just over 300 miles. Prepaid by a 10¢ 1847 stamp on February 21, 1850, the cover was promptly re-addressed back to Albion (less than 300 miles from Albany) and prepaid with a 5¢ stamp on February 25.

France (compared with 42 5¢) and a greater number known used to the British Isles. Shown on this page is an early use (August 12, 1847) from Cumberland, Maryland, to Cumberland, England. There also are 10¢ 1847 covers known used to Germany (four), Belgium (one), Mexico (two from the United States), Cuba and Hawaii, plus a few dozen used from foreign countries, chiefly Canada and Peru.

Most of the 1847 issue covers mailed abroad were sent only partially prepaid. Often the sender paid domestic postage to the border. The ocean postage to the destination could be paid in cash by the recipient in 1847. On the cover in the accompanying photo, for instance, 1 shilling — represented by the black squiggly mark — was due.

Bisected uses of the U.S. 10¢ 1847 stamp on cover are popular and expensive, but not so rare as one might think. About 80 genuine examples are known today. Back in June 1931, proof and essay expert Clarence W. Brazer listed 44 genuine bisect covers plus a few fakes, the latter carefully "tied" with fake handstamps (*Mekeel's Weekly Stamp News*, June 22, 1931).

The most important single source of bisects was the Evans correspondence from Gardiner, Maine — a hoard found, I believe, in Vermont. It consisted of 28 bisect covers, a few of which were badly damaged. Six or seven ratty examples were destroyed, according to stamp dealer Ezra Cole. The covers are addressed to Mrs. George Evans of Brattleboro, Vermont.

Ten-cent bisect covers resulted from lack of 5¢ stamps at certain small post offices, postal historians maintain. The scarcest variety is the horizontal half used as 5¢ on cover. There was one example in the Miller

A 10¢ 1847 stamp on a cover from Cumberland, Maryland, to Cumberland, England. One shilling postage was collected from the recipient.

collection in the New York Public Library. Perhaps one other genuine use is known.

Shown are two covers bearing vertical bisects of the 10¢ 1847. As can be seen from the composite photo of the two half stamps, the bisects were originally the same stamp, which was severed and used as two 5¢ stamps, on covers to different destinations, both posted February 25, 1851. This remarkable reconstruction is the only instance in which vertical bisects of a 10¢ 1847 have been reunited. Diagonal reconstructions also exist, from the aforementioned Gardiner, Maine, find.

About a dozen full covers are known showing 5¢ and 10¢ 1847 stamps used together. A fine example, illustrated on page 29, bears a strip of three 5¢ 1847 and two 10¢ 1847 stamps used on cover from Baltimore to Halifax, Nova Scotia, August 22, 1848. The stamps pay double ocean postage (two times 12¢) plus 10¢ domestic postage from Baltimore to Boston, totaling 34¢, a 1¢ overpay. In addition, 1 shilling is due for British postage for retaliatory rate charges. The retaliatory rate period

This composite photo shows that the bisects on the covers below were originally the same 10¢ 1847 stamp.

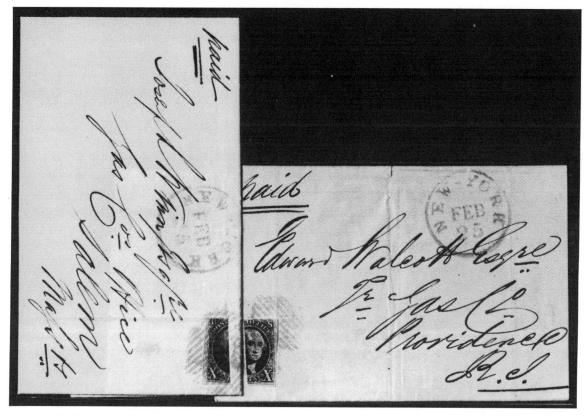

A remarkable reconstruction: two halves of the same 10¢ 1847 stamp, used the same day to pay the 5¢ rate to two different destinations. This is the only instance in which vertical bisects of the 10¢ 1847 have been reunited. The severed halves are shown together in the photo above.

A straightline STEAM marking on a 10¢ 1847 cover directed to New Orleans.

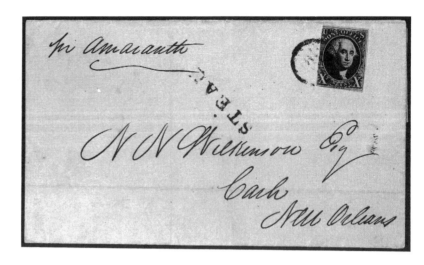

ran from June 27, 1848 to January 3, 1849.

Several covers are known used to Scotland during this period, showing 35¢ postage paid by a single 5¢ 1847 and three 10¢ 1847 Washingtons.

One reason for the scarcity of 5¢ and 10¢ combination covers was the elimination, on March 15, 1849, of triple and other odd-numbered rates. At that time, the United States did away with triple rates to conform with the rating system adopted by Great Britain.

Ten-cent 1847s are known used with locals and with carrier stamps, but such combinations are quite scarce. The 10¢ used with the 1¢ Blood's local, notably Scott 15L17, is perhaps the example most often found. The photo on the opposite page shows a 10¢ 1847 with a Blood's local on cover originating in Philadelphia and sent to Albion, Illinois, on May 10, 1849. A 10¢ is known used on cover with a Charleston, South Carolina, 2¢ yellow Honour's City Express carrier (4LB2) plus a Wilmington & Raleigh circular datestamp. This was a terminal postmark used by railroad route agents.

The 10¢ 1847 is found used on cover with railroad markings. In 1978 Hart reported 152 1847 covers showing railroad markings (*Chronicle 99*), most of them genuine. At last report, about 36 different railroad postmarks are known used on cover with the 1847s.

The late Charles L. Towle, an authority on railroad postal history, remarked in *Chronicle 84* that "railroad markings . . . especially with the 10¢ 1847, command very high prices and a featured position in collections and auction catalogs." As compiled by Towle in 1974, the list of 10¢ 1847 covers with railroad route agent markings totaled just 40. The list was limited to covers showing a railroad route agent marking as the only indication of origin. The most common of these — if any could be termed that — are Wilmington & Raleigh (eight) and Baltimore RR (five).

Towle noted that "all 1847 covers with railroad route agent markings (the list also included 300 5¢ 1847 covers) have not yet been recorded." Markings from such routes as Pennsylvania RR and New Haven & Springfield should exist, he concluded.

One of the more unusual markings to appear on 1847 stamps is the Wheeling, Virginia, red corner grid. This special marking is not a cancellation but a control marking, it is now generally believed, used by the postmaster there to keep track of the 10¢ and 5¢ 1847 stamps. Of course there was no West Virginia at that time: Wheeling was in Virginia. West Virginia did not become a state until 1863. The postmaster used the control grid on the first shipment of 1847 stamps only.

The earliest known cover, I believe, is September 1, 1847. The latest is March 2, 1848. Only two covers are known with the 5¢ 1847 and Wheeling control grid. At least four are known with the 10¢ 1847. There are also five covers from Wheeling, Virginia, with 1847s and no control grid. About seven off-cover 5¢ 1847s and two 10¢ 1847s with Wheeling control grids exist.

Authorities have estimated that fewer than one out of every 400 1847 stamps issued remains on cover. This would suggest the existence of about 10,000 5¢ 1847 covers and 2,500 10¢ covers, roughly speaking. As noted, during the period of use of 1847 adhesives, there were 50 to 100 times as many stampless covers as those

A 10¢ 1847 along with a Blood's local stamp on an 1849 cover from Philadelphia to Illinois.

bearing stamps.

The 1847 stamps were demonetized after June 30, 1851, but a few 10¢ 1847 stamps, like the one on an 1861 cover in the Ishikawa collection, were used and accepted after that date. It seems that the postmaster general's order that 5¢ and 10¢ 1847 stamps "will not be received in prepayment of postage after the 30th of June (1851)" was almost universally ignored, at least by postal officials. The populace began using other issues as they appeared. September 1851 was the deadline for redemption of the 1847 stamps for cash.

Sometimes these illegal late uses of 1847 5¢ or 10¢ stamps are hard to spot. A year-date postal marking, manuscript notation or enclosure is usually a giveaway, barring forgeries or docketing errors made by senders or recipients of the covers. Once in a while the cover franked with 1847 stamps has a postmark or other marking known used only after the date of 1847 stamp demonetization. Other times, as in the case of the Ishikawa cover, the 1847 stamp is accompanied by stamps of later issues.

At least two covers are known whereon the postmasters refused to accept (and so noted) the demonetized 1847 stamps as prepayment of postal charges. One is a 5¢ 1847 used at Kalamazoo, Michigan, in October 1851.

The 1847 stamps were sent to 30 states, three territories, to Washington, D.C., and to Panama. The territories were Minnesota, Wisconsin and the Indian Territory. Territorial 1847 uses are rare. In fact there is only one 10¢ 1847 known used from Minnesota Territory, but no 5¢ 1847 covers. The 10¢ cover has not been seen since 1927. For some years, only one 10¢ 1847 was known from Wisconsin Territory; now there are several.

Some state uses are rare, such as the 10¢ from Delaware. No 10¢ 1847 covers are yet recorded from Iowa. And only three 10¢ 1847s exist used from New Hampshire. However, 11 of the 10¢ bisect covers are known used from that state.

Five major cities received supplies of 1847 stamps during the first 16 days of July: New York (July 1); Boston (July 2); Philadelphia (July 7); Washington (July 9); and Baltimore (July 16). Others waited. New Orleans, for example, had none until August 27. New York City received $5,000 worth of 1847 stamps, but many of the others got just $100 worth.

The 1847 stamps lack the great variety of fancy cancellations found, say, on the 1869 issue or Bank Note stamps. The New York City square grid in red is perhaps the most commonly found type. However, the 1847s do boast some distinctive types. Prominent among these are the St. Johnsbury, Vermont, scarab; the Binghamton, New York, herringbone; and the "TROY & NEW YORK STEAM BOAT," all found on the 10¢ 1847.

As noted in Chapter 1, the zigzag herringbone of Binghamton has been faked on the 1847 stamps. There are at least seven 10¢ 1847 covers known with this fancy Binghamton cancel, but five have been found to be not genuine by experts. One authority believes that none of the known 10¢ 1847s on cover with Binghamton herringbones is genuine. Although red is the most common color of this special cancel, it is found in other colors. Black was used on the fake 10¢ covers.

Two 10¢ 1847 covers are known with the distinctive "TROY & NEW YORK STEAM BOAT" boxed two-line postmark. These are in blue. One of these covers also has a "STEAMER 10" in an oval.

There is confusion about the markings steamboat (or steam), steamship and ship. The marking "STEAMBOAT" is found on mail going via inland waterway or coastal boats, vessels with no mail contract with the Post Office. It is to be distinguished from markings on mail carried by inland or coastal vessels with government mail contracts. "STEAM" or "STEAMBOAT" markings are found, though rarely, on covers with 1847 stamps. The photo on page 26 shows a 10¢ 1847 cover bearing the straightline "STEAM" marking.

"SHIP" markings indicate covers carried by an ocean-going ship. Steamship markings were often used on mail

This retaliatory rate cover from Baltimore to Nova Scotia is franked with three 5¢ and two 10¢ 1847 stamps.

An attractive right sheet margin copy of the 10¢ 1847 stamp, with red grid cancel.

to and from Panama, California and the Caribbean, carried by oceangoing vessels along routes considered post roads. Such steamship markings are also seldom seen on 1847 covers, and then only on late-dated covers beginning in 1850.

New York steamboat markings are found on mail carried on the Hudson River and on lakes Erie and Champlain. Steamboat strikes serve as origin markings as well as accounting tools. Typically, a 2¢ per piece fee was paid to the boat captain for his non-contract service. The "SHIP" marking is typically seen on mail of foreign origin carried by private ship. It is rarely seen on covers with the 1847 issue.

While on the subjects of cancellations on the 10¢ 1847 and postal markings on 10¢ covers, I might say that choice used copies of the 10¢ 1847 are always in demand. It doesn't matter if the stamp bears one of the more prosaic grid killers.

At the height of the speculative fever in certain U.S. stamps and covers during the years 1979-81, choice used copies of the 10¢ stamp, with large margins, brought prices up to $10,000 at auction. (The Scott 1990 retail catalog value is $1,400.) A very pretty used copy, with right sheet margin and a red grid cancel, is shown. Grid cancels on the 10¢ 1847 come in a variety of colors and make an interesting album page if you can afford it. Red, blue and black are the three most common colors. Other colors include orange, magenta, violet, pink, green and ultramarine. I have yet to see the violet, pink or ultramarine, and would have to say they are extremely rare.

Town strikes on the 10¢ 1847 are scarcer than grids. Town strikes reportedly are known in red, blue, black, magenta, orange, and green — all of which I have encountered — but also in violet and ultramarine, which, if they exist, are rare.

There are also special markings, some of which are found on the stamps and have been discussed previously. These include "Paid," "Free," Railroad, U.S. Ex-

The four double transfer types. The faulty transfers, which are difficult to reproduce photographically, generally show most clearly in the letters "U" and "S."

A   B   C   D

press Mail, "Way," numeral, "Steam," "Steamship," "Steamboat," "Steamer 10," Canada, Panama (straightline), and pen or manuscript.

Turning to printing varieties, we find four double transfers, A, B, C and D, listed and described, too briefly, in *Scott's Specialized Catalogue of United States Stamps*. Used examples of all four double-transfer positions are illustrated. When I say described "too briefly," I mean just that. For example, double transfer A, position 1R (first position, upper left corner of the right pane of 100), is described in Scott as "double transfer in 'X' at lower right." But the doubling also occurs in the letters "U" and "S" at the top, as well as in "POST OFFICE." Doubling can also be found in the "S" in "CENTS" and elsewhere. These other distinguishing characteristics are important because double transfer C, position 2R, shows doubling in the "X" at the lower right, the "ENTS" of "CENTS" and in most of the letters in "POST" and "OFFICE" at the top, not to mention the "U" and "S." A careful look at the illustrations in Scott is usually necessary to determine which double transfer you have. While quite distinctive in

1RI (A)

31R1 (B)

2R1 (C)

41RI (D)

The four double transfer types of the 10¢ 1847: 1RI (A), double transfer in "X" at lower right, also in "U" and "S" at top, as well as "POST OFFICE"; 31R (B), double transfer in "POST OFFICE"; 2RI (C), double transfer in "X" at lower right, the "ENTS" of "CENTS" and in most of the letters in "POST" and "OFFICE"; and 41RI (D), double transfer of left and bottom frameline.

31

A large die trial color proof of the 10¢ 1847, with its distinctive cross-hatching, made from the original 1847 die.

real life, these transfer varieties are difficult to reproduce photographically. They may not show clearly in the photo on page 30; the sketches on page 31 are a better guide.

The short-transfer-at-top variety no longer carries a price premium in Scott. Elliott Perry was one of many who objected to this term being used to describe the faintness in the design at the top of certain examples of the 10¢ stamp. Rather, he agreed with Dr. Carroll Chase's explanation that the defect was caused by carelessness in cleaning up or burnishing the plate, i.e., removing the rough burr at the top (or bottom) of the design, made up of metal displaced by the action of the transfer roll. Perry concluded that the cleaning up took place after the recutting; therefore, it might account for some of the "short transfers."

It should be noted that the color and impression of the 10¢ stamp is fairly uniform. Only a few more than 5,000 impressions were taken from the 10¢ plate. The original 1847 plates of 200 impressions were machined off. The plates were then probably used for other jobs, Creighton Hart, 1847 section editor of *The Chronicle*, has stated. Hart and others, however, believe that the original dies were not destroyed in 1851, but were retained and may be buried today in some government repository or private firm's storeroom. As Hart stated in *Chronicle 117*: "The original dies must have been kept by Rawdon, Wright, & Edson and are the ones used in all the late printings. No duplicate dies were made . . . The original dies must be stored safely someplace and they are historically so important that they should be exhibited in the Philatelic Room at the Smithsonian or some equally prominent place." The "someplace," Hart suggests, may be the facilities of the American Bank Note Company.

Illustrated is a large die trial color proof (violet) on bond paper, made from the original 1847 die.

Chapter 3

1875 Reproductions of 1847 Stamps

Date of Issue: 1875
Earliest Known Use: Not valid
for postal use
Scott Catalog Number: 3
Format: Plate of 50 subjects
Designer: Unknown
Engraver: Charles K. Burt
Printer: U.S. Bureau of Engraving
and Printing
Quantity Printed: 11,450
Quantity Issued: 4,779

Date of Issue: 1875
Earliest Known Use: Not valid
for postal use
Scott Catalog Number: 4
Format: Plate of 50 subjects
Designer: Unknown
Engraver: Charles K. Burt
Printer: U.S. Bureau of Engraving
and Printing
Quantity Printed: 10,000
Quantity Issued: 3,883

The 5¢ and 10¢ reproductions of the 1847 stamps are neither fish nor fowl. But they occupy positions three and four in the standard catalogs and must be reckoned with, if for no other reason than that.

The government created these reproductions for display at the 1876 Centennial Exposition held in Philadelphia. The Bureau of Engraving and Printing engraved a single new die, which reproduced the designs of the 5¢ and 10¢ 1847 stamps. Thus, the 1875 stamps are official imitations. From this die, plates were made from which were printed 11,450 impressions of the 5¢ and 10,000 of the 10¢. The reproductions were printed from plates of 50 subjects, arranged 10 across and five rows deep. They were issued imperforate on slightly bluish, ungummed paper. They were not authorized for postal use. Perhaps a few used copies got through, but most used examples bear fake cancels. No covers are recorded.

Why were new dies and plates made? It seems that in 1875 the government was not aware of the existence of, or could not obtain, the original dies (or the plates) used to print the 1847 stamps. As noted, some specialists now believe the 1847 dies still existed in 1875 and may still exist today, buried in the files or storage facilities of either the American Bank Note Company or the United States Government itself. A detailed discussion of this point, by Creighton C. Hart, may be found in the *The Chronicle of the U.S. Classic Postal Issues*, February 1983.

Only 4,779 5¢ Franklin imitations and 3,883 10¢ Washingtons were sold. The rest, apparently unsold remainders, were destroyed.

Scott's 1990 U.S. Specialized catalog lists these two items as 3 (the 5¢ Franklin) and 4 (10¢ Washington), and prices them unused at $850 and $1,000, respectively. These valuations are down drastically from the prices in the 1983 Specialized catalog, $2,000 and $2,500, respectively.

Do these reproductions look like the originals? Yes and no. To the untrained eye they appear similar. But, placed side by side, the differences, while not blatantly obvious, are easily discernible. Let's look at some differences for each value. First the 5¢ Franklin:

At the lower left of the oval, the white shirt frill touches the frame of the oval on a level with the top of the figure "5," while on the 1847 original the frill is lower and lines up with the right serif at the top of the F in FIVE. I have always found this differentiating point confusing both in the telling and the understanding. More significant is the right leg of the N in CENTS. On the reproduction this comes to a point at the bottom, while on the 1847 stamp it is blunt. In *The United States Postage Stamps of the 19th Century,* Lester G. Brookman noted that the reproduction 5¢ is "slightly shorter and a trifle wider than the original" and the "initials 'R.W. H. & E.' at the bottom of the stamp are indistinct instead of clear." But these pointers only help in side-by-side comparisons, if then.

For the 10¢ Washington:

Again, the right leg of the N of CENTS is blunt at the foot on the 1847 and pointed on the reproduction. Another sure test: On the 10¢ 1847 the rectangles of black between the lower serifs (feet) of the left and right "X" are virtually the same size. On the 1875 reproduction, the black shaded area is noticeably fatter at the base of the left than the right "X." Still another test: In the upper left corner of the original 10¢, the U (in US) is rounded and well-formed at the bottom. On the reproduction the lower curve of the U has a flat spot near the O of POST.

Thus, you can forget about trying to detect the "sleepy look" (see Brookman) in the eyes of the reproduction Washington. Nor do you have to examine the coat collar to see whether or not it is shady, shabby or dirty. For the record, Brookman also notes that on the repro-

A full sheet of 50 of the 1875 reproduction of the 5¢ 1847.

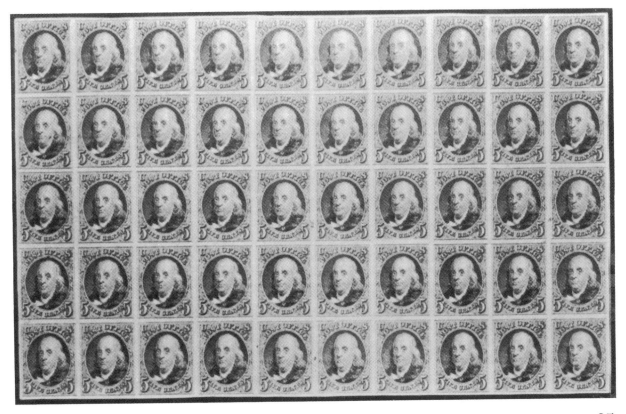

duction there are five horizontal lines between the CE of CENTS and the lower line of the vignette's oval, while there are only four lines there on the 1847 stamp — a difficult-to-discern distinction at best.

Full sheets of both values of the reproductions existed until recently. These reportedly unique sheets of 50 stamps each were auctioned in the Robert Siegel rarity sale in 1976. They sold for $110,000 to Pennsylvania dealer Irwin Weinberg, who subsequently broke them up into blocks of four and six. The catalog description: "The most fabulous set of United States sheets known, an extremely fine and staggering exhibition page (We can find no record of even a set of blocks having been offered in the past 30 or so years) — catalogue value, $70,250." Blocks were soon to come. I might note here that the full sheets of these stamps had only ample margins with no giant selvage.

Complete sheets of 50 of the plate proof on card also exist for both values. A set of sheets, extra fine, cataloging $31,000, sold for $20,000 plus 10-percent buyer's commission at the 1983 Siegel rarity sale. These proof sheets have quite large selvage all around, as wide in some places as the height of a stamp.

Full India paper proof sheets of the 5¢ and 10¢ are

A full sheet of 50 of the 1875 reproductions of the 10¢ 1847.

still extant as well.

Remarkably, at one time a single collector, Mose Iacino of Denver, owned all the sheet sets — the reproductions themselves, the card proofs and the India paper proofs, according to Lester Brookman. Framelines of all positions for both values were recut on the plates because the lines on the dies were rather weak. Some of the recutting on the 10¢ was done sloppily, resulting in irregular framelines.

As stated, the die used for the reproductions contained images of both values, the two engravings being about 18 1/2 millimeters apart. Impressions are known from this dual die showing both stamp designs. An example was in the Crawford collection. It was printed in green on India paper, then mounted on card.

Besides large and small die proofs and plate proofs on both India and cardboard (made in 1875), there exist trial color proofs of the 5¢ and 10¢ reproductions. The 5¢ is known in dull rose lake (plate on card), black and green (both large die). The 10¢ is found in green (large die and India plate). Trial color proofs were made of the 5¢ and 10¢ for the International Cotton Exhibition in Atlanta, Georgia. The set is in five colors on card: black, scarlet, brown, green and blue. Also, in 1912 a special set of small die proofs were printed in very limited quantities on white India paper for exhibit at the Panama Pacific Exposition in San Francisco.

The 10¢ Washington imitation is known printed on bluish vertically laid paper. It may be unique. It was sold in the 1972 Siegel rarity sale for $600.

Up until August 1981, 156 copies of the 5¢ 1847 reproduction and 180 of the 10¢ had been submitted to the Philatelic Foundation for examination. Of these, 145 of the 5¢ and 161 of the 10¢ (93 percent and 89 percent, respectively) were found to be genuine. A few of the 10¢ had been repaired. A small quantity were determined to be proofs.

Chapter 4

1851-57 1¢ Franklin

Date of Issue: July 1, 1851 (types I, Ib, II, IIIa)

Type Ia: April 1857

Type III: December 1855 (position 99R2); April 1857 (plate 4 examples)

Type IV: May (?), 1852

Earliest Known Use: Type I: July 5, 1851

Type Ib: July 1, 1851 (Boston)

Type Ia: April 19, 1857

Type II: July 1, 1851 (plate 1); December 5, 1855 (plate 2)

Type III: Unknown

Type IIIa: 1851 (plate 1E examples);

1855-56 (plate 2); 1857 (plate 4)

Type IV: June 8, 1852 (Scott)

Scott Catalog Numbers: 5 (type I), 5A (type Ib), 6 (type Ia), 7 (type II), 8 (type III), 8A (type IIIa), 9 (type VI)

Format: Two panes of 100

Designer: Edward Purcell

Engravers: Joseph Ives Pease (portrait), Henry Earle (border and lettering)

Printer: Toppan, Carpenter, Casilear & Company of Philadelphia

Quantity Issued: Type I: 30,000 estimated (Brookman)

Type Ib: 180,000 estimated

Types Ia, II, III, IIIa, IV: unknown

For many collectors, the U.S. 1¢ Franklin imperforate stamps of 1851-57 are too expensive and too complex to tackle. There is much justification for this. Getting a grasp of these lovely blue engraved stamps requires knowledge and some basic facts. And obtaining any of them requires money. For several varieties, "money" translates into very much money. In this chapter, the collector will, I hope, gain some insight into why these stamps are worth having, even to the extent of scrimping on the family's grocery bill.

The imperforate type I 1¢ Franklin comes from just one position on one plate.

The 1¢ blue imperforate Franklins (Scott 5, 5A, 6, 7, 8, 8A and 9) were printed from four plates, 1 through 4. Each plate had 200 positions, divided into two panes of 100 subjects each, arranged 10 by 10. Between the left and right panes was a dividing center line. Plate 1's 200 positions were re-entered and/or recut. That is, some lines of engraving were added or strengthened. This produced a second state (condition) of the plate, which we term plate 1 late as opposed to plate 1 early.

These five plates produced the four primary types of the 1¢ Franklin imperforates: I, II, III and IV, corresponding to Scott 5, 7, 8 and 9. Plate 1 produced all the type I and Ib stamps, the latter an important subtype. Plate 4 produced all the type Ia stamps, a second major subtype. Three plates, 1 early, 2 and 4, produced the third major listed subtype, type IIIa. Type III stamps were produced by plate 2 (only position 99 of the right pane) and 4.

For the specialist there is another subtype, Ic. This comes from plate 4, which perhaps is the most interesting of the five.

For the collector of U.S. classic issues — those issued prior to 1894 — Scott 5, the type I (position 7, right pane, plate 1, early state) presents a formidable set of difficulties: availability and price. The type I stamp comes from just that one position on plate 1 early, issued July 1, 1851. The example illustrated has an unusually good bottom margin. There are today in existence only some 80 to 90 examples of this stamp in all conditions. The late Mortimer L. Neinken stated in June 1984 that only 69 examples, used, unused or on cover, have ever been certified by the Philatelic Foundation. This total includes about four unused copies and 18 on cover. The rarity of this stamp justifies the high catalog prices: $200,000 unused and $17,500 used (1990). Its separate listing makes it a must for the collector of classics who wants completion.

There are other very rare 1¢ imperforate Franklins,

One of four known unused copies of type I, position 7R1E. This is the best of the four. The stamp sold for $57,500 at the Wunderlich sale conducted by Robert A. Siegel Auction Galleries in January 1976.

but none quite so rare and desirable as position 7R1E. The 1¢ Franklin stamps (imperforate and perforated) have challenged some of the greatest philatelists, collectors and accumulators since the early part of this century, and rightfully so. Back in 1922, Stanley B. Ashbrook wrote an article in *The American Philatelist* called "An Analysis of the Types of the U.S. One Cent 1851 and 1857." The article appeared in Volume 35, Number 5, February 1922, and in his foreword he gave credit to two earlier collector-philatelists: John N. Luff and Sir Nicholas E. Waterhouse, both of whom were intensely interested in classic U.S. stamps. Ashbrook also thanked Dr. Carroll Chase, Ernest R. Jacobs and Alvin Good for their help and loans of material Ashbrook needed in his incredible study of the 1¢ Franklin stamps of 1851-60.

What is most interesting is that as long ago as 1922, Ashbrook had assessed most of the problems associated with these stamps. By 1972, when Mortimer Neinken published his marvelous update of the first volume of Ashbrook's two-volume work (published in 1936), most of the work on the 1¢ Franklin imperforates had been done. Collectors then were fortunate, and have continued to be fortunate, in having these wonderful sources for study and collecting.

Yet there are still questions to be answered, plates to be plated and finds to be made. There were other famous collections of the 1¢ Franklin besides Ashbrook's. The Chase, Newbury, Fleckenstein, Neinken and Forscheimer collections come to mind.

But it wasn't until about 1970 that the greatest collection of these stamps came to be formed. Its formation took some 10 years, fed by unlimited funds, many astute agents and a captain whose course was unwavering. The goal: an international Grand Prix award. But it was not to be. Ryohei Ishikawa of Tokyo, Japan, had to put together a mindboggling run of classic United States stamps from 1847 through the 1869 Pictorial issue to attain his goal, achieved in Vienna, Austria, at WIPA 81. This exhibit contained copies of the type I used and on cover and the type III, position 99R2 (more about this stamp later) unused, used and on cover, among other choice tidbits.

After Ishikawa, Roland H. Cipolla II of Florida assembled an international gold medal winning collection of the 1¢ Franklin. And waiting in the wings are collections that may or may not be exhibited, accumulations of the 1¢ Franklin that are in their own right staggering. But

Type I

will the world ever see them? Some, never.

When Scott Stamp and Coin Company published the second edition of the *Specialized Catalogue of United States Stamps* in 1924, the 1¢ blue Franklin (number 30 in the catalog then) was priced at $1,750 unused and $225 used. It was not priced on cover. In the 1990 Scott catalog, the prices are $200,000, $17,500 and $25,000 for unused, used and on cover, respectively. What this says is that this stamp has long been recognized as a major variety and major rarity and continues to go up in price. The demand is large; the supply is small with only about 90 copies known. The photo on this page shows this rare stamp as the left item in the pair. The right stamp is type Ib.

No more than 30,000 copies of this stamp could have been printed between the spring of 1851 and the time the plate was altered, probably late in 1851, so that it no longer produced type I stamps. So, if some 90 survive today, then just one in 333 or only .003 percent have endured. There are fewer of them around today than the fabled 24¢ inverted airplane.

True, the type I, position 7R1E, is just a type example of a design, the 1¢ Franklin imperforate. But it is the only position that shows the full die design with almost complete ornaments at top, bottom and both sides. For the stamp to be position 7R1E, it must show this virtually complete design as well as the characteristic double transfer of the design, especially noticeable in the upper right corner and the top label letters "U.S. POSTAGE."

As Neinken noted in *The United States One Cent Stamp of 1851 to 1861*, published in 1972 by the U.S.

A rare pair of 1¢ Franklin stamps of 1851. The left stamp is position 7R1E, the only true type I imperforate. The other is one of the two best examples of type Ib, position 8R1E.

A type Ia Scott 6 stamp showing the complete design at the bottom but cut away at the top.

Philatelic Classics Society, page 58: "When the re-entry of this position was attempted, the re-entered relief was to the right of the original entry. The background lines of the right part of the medallion (see illustration) extended into the design at the right. Pronounced doubling exists in the upper right corner ornament, proving the re-entry of the type I relief and not the trimmed 'T' relief."

Con artists have attempted to make realistic-looking copies of the imperf type I. Sometimes they do it by inking in full bottom plumes and scrolls on a type II stamp. On one of the more skillful attempts, the faker did his work on the bottom stamp in a pair, and the true type I stamp, of course, is from the top row! More often the faker will try to pass off a perforated type I (by trimming off the perfs) or the 1875 reprint or a proof of it. But he must remove the "secret mark," a dot of color in the left center portion of the white oval around the Franklin vignette. Not only does this usually leave evidence of removal, but the stamp will not show the characteristic double transfer at the upper right corner.

There are two outstanding items that show the imperf type I stamp at its best. Both are illustrated on page 76 of Neinken's book. The first is the largest known piece containing position 7R1E: an irregular unused block of eight. It comprises positions 4R1E to 9R1E in the top row and 14-15R1E below. The rare type I includes part of the top sheet margin and is just touched at one point at the bottom corner plume. The second item is the most beautiful type I cover known (of the 18 recorded by Neinken). This is the ex-Saul Newbury cover from Richmond, Virginia, to New York City, now in the Ishikawa collection. It is franked with a horizontal strip of three 1¢ Franklins, position 7-9R1E, having full margins all around. Each stamp is struck with a neat red grid cancel. The cover was mailed July 5, 1851, just five days after the 1851 stamps were released.

In 1980, Sotheby Parke Bernet Auction Company sold for $39,600 a cover bearing a vertical strip of three from plate 1E, positions 7, 17 and 27R1E, tied by bright red grids. The fillip was a matching red Louisville & Cincinnati Mail Line postmark dated March 8. The type I has a sealed tear. The destination of the cover: Philadelphia. It is ex-Dr. Carroll Chase.

Still another strip of three cover with the type I was in the Emmerson Krug collection. This beauty is illustrated in Volume I of *The United States Postage Stamps of the 19th Century*, by Lester G. Brookman, page 113. The

Flaw

Type Ia

strip is from position 6-8R1E, types Ib, I, Ib, the most desirable types to have together, as we shall see. This cover traveled from North Cumberland, Pennsylvania, to Milton (Wilton?), Virginia.

On page 75 of Neinken's book, there is an illustration of the only known on-cover pair containing types I and Ib. The cover is a folded circular, dated March 1852, used from New Haven, Connecticut, to Columbus, Ohio.

As would be expected, the great collection of Alfred Caspary had a 7R1E cover. It was a large-margined single tied by a blue Philadelphia, Pennsylvania, postmark to a small printed circular to Newburgh, New York, in February 1852. When the cover was sold by Harmers of New York in 1956, it cataloged $1,500. An appreciative collector snared it for $2,600. The mystique of great collections continues.

The Robert A. Siegel 1968 Rarities of the World sale included a type I single plus two other 1¢ Franklins on a cover that also originated in Philadelphia. The cover was addressed to "U.S. Arsenal, Pikeville, Maine." (Maine postal historians, does this pique your interest?) There also is a red star carrier cancel on the cover. The type I is cut into or close at the top and bottom, as is the type Ib. Stanley B. Ashbrook checked over this cover and gave it his imprimatur. It sold for a reasonable $2,700 against a then catalog value of $4,845.

Some other type I covers include a single on cover with a North Ogdensburgh, New York, "RR" 1852 postmark. The stamp is fine, slightly cut into. In 1982 it sold for $23,100 at a Richard Wolffers auction. The stamp is tied by a "NEW YORK 1 Ct." A strip of three, 6-8R1E with close margins to slightly cut in, appeared in the 1967 Siegel Rarities sale. It was sent from Boston to Georgetown, D.C. The cover realized $4,200 against a catalog value of $5,000. A strip of three from positions 5-7R1E was in the 1975 Siegel Rarities sale. The type Ib, Ib, I strip was tied by blue "SKANEATELES NY" 1852 postmarks. It sold for "only" $3,250, due to the tops of the stamps being cut into. In the 1968 H.R. Harmer auction of the Barrett G. Hindes collection, lot 31 was a 7-9R1E strip on a November 21, 1851, cover from St. Louis to Galena, Illinois. The strip had small to large margins. The cover was ex-Richey and signed by Ashbrook.

The type Ib stamp is not quite as rare as type I, but is a very rare and valuable stamp nonetheless. Like the type I, type Ib stamps come only from the top row of the right pane of plate 1 in its early state. Position 7R1E is

Type Ib

type I; positions 3, 4, 5, 6, 8 and 9R1E are type Ib. If there are some 90 type I stamps known, then perhaps about 500 type Ib stamps exist. Possibly the number is a lot less.

No perforated type Ib stamps can exist. That makes it simple: only imperforate, only six possible positions, all identifiable from the Neinken or Ashbrook books.

Stamps from plate 1E were used approximately during the period from July 1, 1851, to May or June 1852. Like the others, they were manufactured (printed) by the firm of Toppan, Carpenter, Casilear & Company. They were no longer valid anywhere for postage as of January 1862. Usage was permitted as late as December 31, 1861, in California and Oregon and in the territories of New Mexico, Utah and Washington (*Chronicle* 122, p. 118).

The discussion concerning type I stamps on cover relates to the type Ib, as these came from the same top row of the right pane of plate 1E Any horizontal multiple containing a type I stamp must contain one or more type Ib stamps also. As I mentioned, they come from positions 3, 4, 5, 6, 8 and 9. Because positions 6R1E and 8R1E (the stamps flanking type I) show the type characteristics best (have the most complete design) they rate the highest prices and are the most eagerly sought by collectors. As a matter of fact, they receive separate prices in the Scott Specialized catalog.

The type Ib stamps show the bottom scrolls and corner plumes almost — but not quite — complete. At the top and the sides, however, their designs are complete as on the type I. Type Ia stamps show complete ornaments at the bottom as type I, but the top ornaments and top outer frameline are noticeably cut away.

Rule of thumb: A type Ib is a type I at top; a type Ia is a type I at bottom.

The type Ia stamp, Scott 6, is nothing less than a "mean critter." It seldom comes in extra-fine condition — even if you can find one — and always sells for more than catalog price in choice condition. But it is a "must" stamp for the specialist in U.S. imperforate classic stamps.

All type Ia stamps come from the bottom row of plate 4. They are found in 18 of the 20 bottom row positions. Positions 91 and 96R4 are "almost" type Ia. Their design is much more complete than type IIIa (which we'll get to later). Specialists call this intermediate design type Ic.

Why are there so many types of the 1851-57 1¢ Franklin? Most of the type designations come from the amount of the original design trimmed off, at top, bottom and/or the sides. Why was all that trimming done? Probably because the original design was just too tall for a column of 10 stamp designs to fit on the plate with any space left between them so they could be cut apart. Plate 4 may be the best example of this. Top row plate 4 stamps have very complete designs at the bottom. Most stamps from the interior of plate 4 are noticeably trimmed at the top, bottom or both. So type Ia stamps — from the bottom row of plate 4 — look like type I at the bottom but are quite cut away at top. The accompanying photo shows an excellent example of a type Ia stamp.

The relief used to enter plate 4's bottom row (as well as the sixth row, positions 51-60L and R) had a small flaw in it. This flaw is a short colorless horizontal dash below

The bottom stamps in this very rare unused block of the 1¢ Franklin are type Ia. The arrow points to the relief flaw that all type Ia stamps must have.

Type Ic

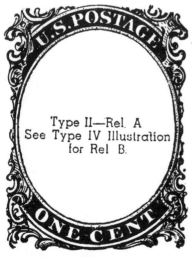

Type II

the "U" of "U.S." The cancel on the illustrated single stamp (page 42) partly covers it. You can see it better on the bottom pair of the block of four on page 45. An arrow points to the flaw on the right stamp. All type Ia stamps have this flaw. However, type Ic stamps and some type III and IIIa stamps also can have it. So if the flaw is not there, it can't be a type Ia; if the flaw is there, it may be a type Ia.

Mention of the type Ic demands an explanation here. These are in limbo, but are rare and desirable to specialists. Type Ic stamps come from eight positions on plate 4. On page 266 of Neinken's book, he quotes Ashbrook regarding the type Ic stamps: "Six of the eight came from the E relief, but two came from the bottom row and originated from the F relief, the true type IA."

Type Ic and type Ia are identical except in one respect. Both have the bottom left plume (at the extreme bottom left corner) complete. On type Ic, however, the bottom right plume is almost — but not quite — complete. Type Ia has both plumes totally complete.

On May 17, 1961, Robert A. Siegel sold a portion of the Saul Newbury collection of outstanding U.S. stamps. A superb used type Ia, position 99R4 with large margins and a light black cancel, sold for $675 against a catalog value of just $250. In the 1984 Siegel Rarities of the World auction, a very-fine used copy, cut so the scrollwork at left was touched, sold for $6,050 against a catalog of $3,500 ($6,500 in 1990). The market today perhaps is trailing the catalog for a copy with the design intact. Scott lists a used copy at $6,500 and an unused one at $20,000. Mint examples are scarce.

It should be noted that the reason type Ia and Ic stamps are so uncommon is that imperforate sheets from plate 4 were issued only during April and May of 1857 and probably during part of June. By July, sheets were being perforated. This produced Scott 19 and 22 varieties, the perforated types Ia and Ic, respectively. There are more perforated multiples of type Ia than imperforate. Imperf blocks containing type Ia stamps are very rare. A unique block of six from the ninth and tenth rows of plate 4 did exist. According to Lester Brookman, it still may be intact. The block on page 45 is a beautiful unused block. The bottom two stamps are type Ia.

Single copies of type Ia showing the bottom margin are scarce and very desirable also. On page 276 of the Neinken book is illustrated a gem single with an 11 1/2-millimeter bottom sheet margin. The stamp also has a portion of the stamp above attached. It's a real showstopper and worth a great deal more than catalog value.

The accompanying photo shows a wonderful strip of three. It's from positions 80, 90 and 100L4, comprising types IIIa, IIIa and Ia. This gem sold in the Ishikawa auction for a pathetic $4,675 to an informed buyer. The pen cancels destroyed the value in the eyes of many potential bidders.

To recap: The type Ia imperforates come from 18 positions on plate 4. Type Ic stamps come from positions 49L, 83L, 41R, 81R, 82R, 89R, 91R and 96R4. In Neinken's opinion, position 49R4 also is a type Ic. Neinken told me in June 1984, "In my opinion, Stanley Ashbrook should not have originated the type Ic. It only causes problems. Surely positions 91R4 and 96R4 should be listed as type Ia."

In summary, probably there is no reason why type Ic stamps should not rate somewhere close to type Ia stamps in price and desirability. But one needs to have a specialist's or advanced collector's appreciation of the difference. As for shades, Neinken said light blue varieties are scarcer than dark blue.

These rare and expensive stamps are missing from most U.S. collections, even advanced ones. They don't even enter into the thinking of the average collector. But they force the true philatelist to exercise his mind, if not his bank account.

At last we come to a type of the 1¢ Franklin imperforate of 1851 that almost any collector can afford: type II. Unfortunately, type II stamps (Scott 7) often are difficult to identify, especially if viewed alone, without any others for comparison. The relevant language in the Scott Specialized catalog states: "The little balls of the bottom scrolls and the bottoms of the lower plume ornaments are missing. The side ornaments are complete." Shown on page 48 is a typical type II stamp. Note that the outer lines above "POSTAGE" and below "ONE CENT" are complete. There is no break in either line. Also, they're not recut. That would make them look much heavier or darker than the other lines.

Outside of that, about the only way to tell a type II is by what isn't there. The top ornaments aren't as complete as a type I or Ib (although on some type II stamps they are nearly complete). The plumes at the bottom corners are more than half cut away, and the ornaments below the "N" of "ONE" and the "N" of "CENT" do not turn under to form scrolls.

Types IIIa, IIIa and Ia in a strip.

A typical type II can be identified by what it isn't.

The stamp shown here has the top right ornament nearly complete, but remember that one characteristic doesn't change the type. Sometimes the only way to deduce that a stamp is a type II is to eliminate every other type. That can be a long and difficult road, especially if the stamp is cut close.

When I'm asked to type a 1¢ Franklin imperforate, I always hope it isn't a type II. Type II stamps come from five plates: 1E, 1L (just one position, 4R), 2, 3 and 4. From the most common to the rarest, they rank as follows: 2, 1E, 4, 3 and 1L. Plate 1E was issued July 1, 1851; plate 1L, about the middle of 1852; plate 2, 1855; plate 3, early 1856; plate 4, about April 1857.

Some large type II pieces are available today. The Ryohei Ishikawa collection included a pane of 100 from plate R1L. It contained 99 type IV and the lone type II from position 4. Ishikawa also had a complete pane of 100 from the right side of plate 2. This comprised 99 type II and a single type III from position 99 (more on this rare stamp later).

One of the most desirable pieces of imperf type II is shown. It is an unused block of 12 with the "big plate 2 flaw." This is thought to be more than just a plate crack.

This unused block showing most of the "big plate 2 flaw" is one of the outstanding type II pieces known to collectors of classic U.S. stamps.

It was an actual flaw in the plate's surface that broke open and became wider and wider as the plate wore from printing. The block comes from late in the plate's life when the flaw was quite wide. It's amazing that the printers didn't discard the plate or the government refuse to accept such an obviously defective product. Luckily for collectors, neither happened.

One strip that stands out in my mind is that from the Judge Emerson and Captain Barrett Hindes collections. This horizontal strip of three, showing positions 98, 99 and 100R2 (types II, III and IIIa) is very rare. Fortunately, it has been preserved. In the 1968 H.R. Harmer sale of the Hindes collection, it brought $1,700.

Type II stamps were used the most from late 1855 through 1857, but type II covers can be found during the whole period from July 1851 through 1857 and beyond.

As with the imperforate type I 1¢ Franklins, there aren't enough type III stamps to go around. With demand exceeding supply, prices are steep. The standard catalogs list type III stamps in a diminishing order of value, not by any logical plate sequence. Detractors like to yell loudly and clearly that a separate listing for a single position — 99R2 — of one stamp is nonsense. But where does that leave the type I, position 7R1E?

The 99R2 does not have the same mystique and glamor of 7R1E. Very-fine copies bring big prices, but seldom much more than catalog — at least in recent years. As you read the following statements from Stanley Ashbrook and Mortimer Neinken, refer to the 99R2 stamp in the accompanying photo.

"The rare 99R2 is the result of a very decided short transfer in the attempt to re-enter this position, which was rocked with a relief of type II. The short occurs at both top and bottom, and is the cause of both lines being broken. The position above (89R2) was re-entered before 99, but a bad guess was made as to the correct space, resulting in the bottom part of 89R2 occupying the intervening space between 89 and 99. Why 89 was not entirely erased from the plate and a fresh entry made is not known. In order to avoid dropping 99 below the other design in the bottom row, it was simply intentionally shortened."

This passage was taken from the *American Philatelist* way back in February 1922. That is remarkable. Of course, the author has to be Ashbrook. He had stated on the previous page: "As 99R2 is an exception, it should be given a separate listing in the catalogue . . ." Sure enough!

A used copy of the 1¢ blue type III, position 99R2, featuring a New York postmark.

Position 99R2 is considered by specialists to be the best example of type III characteristics on the 1¢ Franklin.

A typical type IIIa showing the outer frameline broken at the top. Some will show a wider break, some a narrower one.

In the 1924 edition of Scott's *Specialized United States* (second earliest), there it is, Number 42, 99R2, type III. It was priced at $350 used; there was no unused price. (The number 42 reflects Scott's old numbering system. Postmasters' provisionals started with Number 1; Number 28 was the 1847 5¢.)

Ashbrook's *An Analysis of the Types of the U.S. One Cent 1851 and 1857*, published more than 60 years ago, proved to be the foundation of his epic 1936 work, *The United States One Cent Stamp of 1851-1857*. Neinken's 1972 revision of Ashbrook's Volume 1 continues this differentiation. It devotes a separate listing to 99R2, "the finest example of type III."

Up to early 1980, 109 alleged examples of 99R2 had been submitted to the Philatelic Foundation in New York City for expertization. Of these, only 38 turned out to be genuine, in the opinion of the PF. A remarkable total of 71 copies had been altered or incorrectly identified by the submitter.

What is the correct identification of type III? It sounds simple: If the outer curved frameline is broken at both top and bottom, the stamp is a type III. There's a catch, though. Not all type IIIs have wide breaks in the framelines. Some are downright tiny. Also, several positions on plate 4 started out as type IIIa: one outer frameline broken but the other complete. (In almost every case, it's the top line that's broken and the bottom one that's not.) As plate 4 wore from printing stamps, some of the faint bottom lines wore away and became incomplete. So it's a very fine line (no pun intended) sometimes between a type IIIa and a type III.

Theoretically, a certain position on a sheet would be type IIIa, and the same position on the next sheet printed would be type III! That gives you an idea of how carefully some stamps must be examined. It also explains why the wider the break, the higher the price (all other things being equal).

Next question: How do you tell a 99R2 (1990 Scott retail price $8,000 unused and $2,750 used) from any other type III ($5,500 unused and $1,500 used)? At the right end of the curved label containing "ONE CENT" is an ornament that looks something like a backward "C." Right above that is a smaller ornament that looks like a frontward "c." It's that top "c" ornament that has the clue that's easiest to spot. It's there that the shifted transfer is easiest to see. That "c" is doubled straight down about two-thirds of its height.

Type III

50

Be careful of any type III you buy. Many a perforated type V has had its perforations removed in order to pass it off as a type III. The type V side ornaments were partly trimmed off to give more room for the perforations. A true type III will have complete or virtually complete side ornaments, especially at the top.

I leave you with this question: Is a 99R2, valuable as it may be due to its rarity, worth a separate catalog listing and that lofty price?

Type III stamps from plate 4 are not nearly as rare as 99R2, considered the best example of the type. But they also are hard to find, expensive, often cut close or defective. They appear almost as infrequently as the less distinct type Ib stamps (positions 3, 4, 5 and 9R1E), which have higher catalog values.

Plate 4 produced stamps beginning about April 1857. Just a few months later, all stamps were being perforated, so imperf type III and IIIa stamps are few and far between. Type III stamps are found much less frequently than those known as type IIIa. Remember, type III stamps have the side ornaments complete but have both the top and bottom outer framelines broken. Type IIIa stamps, by contrast, have either the top or the bottom frameline broken, but not both. Complete side framelines are important. Fakers have been known to cut away the perforations on cheap type V stamps and try to pass these off as the much scarcer type III imperforates.

Only 37 positions out of 200 on plate 4 produced true type III stamps. Blocks of type III or IIIa are very rare, as well as blocks showing a combination of the two types. Imperforate type IIIa stamps also are found on plate 1E.

Late in the life of plate 2, the bottom frameline on position 100R wore away, turning the type II into a IIIa. Therefore, it is possible to have a strip of three, 98-100R2 comprising type II, III (the rare 99R2) and IIIa. Position 100R2 is an unusual type IIIa in another way, too. Nearly every type IIIa has the top line broken. Very few show just the bottom broken.

Plate 4, despite its rather short imperforate life, is remarkable. It contains 37 type III stamps, 18 type Ia, eight to 10 type Ic, more than 100 type IIIa and just 20 of the relatively common type II. No wonder that no one yet has plated its 200 positions by reconstruction. It would take an army of buyers, wheelbarrows of cash and the cooperation of dozens of well-heeled knowledgeable philatelists. Few young collectors can afford to specialize in these very difficult and expensive imperforate Franklins.

An unusual type IIIa with the bottom line broken.

Type IIIa

51

Ashbrook notes that he began reconstruction of plate 4 in 1919 and was still at it more than 17 years later. It's comparable to Sherlock Holmes being on a case for 17 years. Standard catalogs don't help much either. For example, type II stamps from plate 4 are scarce, and the 1990 Scott Specialized catalog gives them no listing unused and a premium price of $500 used compared with the $450 and $85 prices of the most common ones, unused and used respectively. This comes somewhat near reflecting the difference in value between type II stamps from plates 1E and 2 and those from plate 4. Only rarely does one find a type II from plate 4. They come only from the top row, making them nearly as rare as the type Ia stamps from the bottom row. Neinken has called them "scarcer than hens' teeth."

However, there may be hope for an actual complete reconstruction of plate 4.

Neinken told me in 1984 that "the reconstruction of plate 4 is almost complete. A perforated left pane of 100 was used to plate half the positions. For the right pane, I had a perforated block of 28, a used imperforate block of 10, a perforated block of nine and several blocks of four. There are only two or three positions which are doubtful."

We find red, blue and black cancels, carrier, numeral and "PAID" markings on type III and IIIa stamps. I suspect that a few green cancels exist on plate 4 stamps, but I have never seen one. All the different cancellation varieties listed for the imperforate 3¢ stamps lead me to

Position 4-5R1L The left stamp is the only plate 1L stamp not recut and is a type II. The right stamp is recut once at the bottom. Such a pair is scarce.

conclude that the 1¢ cancel variety lists of Brookman and Scott are not all inclusive. In fact, they might be downright incomplete.

Neither type is especially scarce on cover as compared with a used off-cover example. Still, covers are far from common, like the off-cover stamps. Shown is a type IIIa on a local cover paying the 1¢ fee. Many type III and IIIa covers slip by the collector who lacks knowledge or acuteness of observation.

To summarize: Type III has the outer frameline broken at both top and bottom, the best example being position 99 of the right pane of plate 2. Type IIIa stamps have a break in one line but not both, the broken line usually being found at the top. Both types — and all imperforate 1¢ Franklins, for that matter — must have the side ornaments complete or virtually complete.

Typically, if you own just one 1¢ imperforate Franklin of the 1851 issue, it's either a type II or a type IV. If it isn't recut, it's the type II; if it is recut, it's the type IV, the most common and readily available of all the imperforate 1¢ Franklins. Type IV comes from 199 of the 200 positions on plate 1 late. The "late state" refers to the stamps after recutting, which turned types I, Ib, II and IIIa into type IV.

How do recuts come about? An engraver alters (recuts) the designs on the plate with a special tool. On plate 1L, the transfer roll itself was re-entered on some positions. Then the outer framelines at top and bottom were strengthened (engraved more deeply) by hand. Those recut lines hold more ink and so look darker to the eye. Shown is a type IV stamp with the outer line at top and bottom recut. It's easy to see on this example.

There are seven different recut combinations: 113

A typical type IV of the 1¢ Franklin with one line recut at top and one recut at bottom.

A choice type IIIa on a local cover. This is position 79 from the left pane of plate 4.

This diagram shows the remains of the original (inverted) transfer. The heavy diagonal line through the upper left ornament (called the "hook" by specialists) usually is the easiest way to spot the inverted transfer on the 1¢ Franklin.

positions were recut once at top and once at bottom; 40 were recut once at top only; 21 once at top and twice at bottom; 11 recut twice at bottom; eight recut once at bottom only; four twice at top and once at bottom; and just two positions (52L and 79L) recut twice at top and twice at bottom.

You need a good magnifying glass, a keen pair of eyes and some charts to identify all the plate 1 late positions, but it can be done. Acquiring one example of each recut type is enough for most collectors.

A pair containing both types II and IV is very scarce, as it must include position 4R1L, the only type II stamp on the plate. Such a pair is shown on page 52. You may recall that position 4R1E was a type Ib. When the plate was altered, this position was re-entered and lost its Ib characteristics, becoming a type II.

Plate 1L was in use from mid-1852 until at least 1857, so more stamps were printed from it than any other of the imperforate plates. So the most common 1¢ type is found with the widest range of cancels. Green cancels are rare and beautiful, as are some of the packet-boat markings. This stamp also shows what may be the first true precancels. Blocks are available, though rather costly. The 1990 Scott Specialized gives a retail price of $1,500 for an unused block of the type IV, number 9. A type II block (plate 2) lists at $2,100. After that, blocks of any of the other imperf 1¢ are in the stratosphere.

A few type IV stamps were perforated unofficially. They gauge 12 1/2, as opposed to the regular perf 15 of the 1857-60 issue. The few known examples are rare. They catalog $3,000 in Scott.

There also are the scarce and interesting inverted transfers. After the first three positions had been entered on plate 1E (positions 10, 20 and 30 on a printed sheet of stamps) production stopped. Those three designs were mostly removed. Then the plate was turned end for end, and all 200 positions entered fresh. But now, positions 71, 81 and 91 on the printed sheet showed traces of the old entries, in an inverted position. Shown is a diagram of position 91L1L showing the remains of the old transfer. A vertical margin strip containing positions 71, 81 and 91L1L is one of the highlights of any well-developed showing of type IV stamps.

Late printings from plate 1L show the recut lines much more clearly. The reason, said Neinken, is that the "recutting was engraved much deeper than the ornamental parts of the transferred designs." "As the surface of the plate wore down, the lines of the design grew fainter, throwing the deep recut lines in bolder relief," he said. (See page 132 of the Neinken book.)

Don't confuse "dry" printings with worn impressions. Until recently, paper had to be moist for the printing ink to stick to it. Sometimes too much time would elapse between the moistening and printing, and the paper would start to dry. This drying would start at the edges, so dry printings most often occur in the outer rows of the sheet.

Much more could be written about these beautiful blue engraved stamps picturing our first postmaster general — and it has. Read the monumental two-volume book by Ashbrook and Neinken's update of Volume I (printing and plating). Maybe you can discover another copy of 99R2 or 7R1E. (In the early 1980s, an auction describer discovered an unidentified strip of 7-9R1E on cover, catalog value $60,000!)

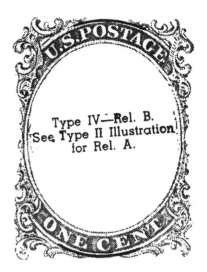

Type IV

Chapter 5

1851 3¢ Washington

Date of Issue: July 1, 1851 (orange brown); 1851 (dull red)

Earliest Known Use: July 1, 1851 (orange brown); October 4, 1851 (dull red by plate); October 22, 1851 (dull red by color)

Scott Catalog Numbers: 10 (orange brown) 11 (dull red)

Format: Two panes of 100

Designer: Edward Purcell

Engravers: Joseph Ives Pease (portrait); Henry Earle (border and lettering)

Printer: Toppan, Carpenter, Casilear & Company of Philadelphia

Quantity Issued: An estimated 362,275,000 Scott 10 and 11 stamps issued; the greater part of the total were dull red stamps.

Despite the fact that the 3¢ Washington stamp of 1851-57 is perhaps the most complex of all United States classic imperforate stamps, many general collectors have found that obtaining a copy of both Scott 10 and 11 is very easy. Get a Washington in the orange-brown shade (Scott 10) and in the dull red or other 1852-57 shades (Scott 11), and that is all there is to it. There are times when the collector or dealer wonders if a specific copy is an orange brown or one of the other shades. This is important because price differences between Scott 10 and 11 are substantial. The first is valued at about seven times more used and nine times more unused than the latter. If you look at the 1990 Scott U.S. Specialized catalog you see: "10, orange brown, type I, $1,000 (unused), $40 (used); 11, dull red, type I, $130 (unused), $7 (used); and 11a, claret, type I, $160 (unused), $10 (used)."

It is inconsistent that the 3¢ Washington is listed and numbered by color rather than by type. True, both 10 and 11 are type I, where there is an outer frameline at all four sides. But the only foolproof method of determining whether you have the scarcer orange-brown shade is through plating (determining which plate printed the stamp by the stamp's characteristics). Scott 10, the orange brown, comes from five plates: 1 early and intermediate states, 2 early, 5 early and 0. Scott 11 comes from eight plates: 1 late, 2 late, 3, 4, 5 late, 6, 7 and 8.

Perhaps the single most important key to plating is to study the recut inner vertical framelines. Dr. Carroll Chase explains this in his landmark work, *The 3¢ Stamp of the United States 1851-1857 Issue.* Does the stamp show both inner vertical lines? If so, it comes from one of nine plates: 0, 1E, 1I (the "I" stands for "intermediate"), 1L, 2E, 2L, 3, 5E or 5L. If it is orange brown, it is from plates 1E, 1I, 2E, 5E or 0. Does the design show no inner vertical lines? Then it comes from one of the following: 1E, 1I, 4, 6, 7, 8. (Some plates produced more than one variety.) The first two were printed only in orange brown. If the stamp has an inner vertical line on one side only, it comes from 1E, 1I, 5E or 5L. The first three produced orange browns. Stamps not in orange brown with a single inner vertical line come from plate 5L.

Orange-brown stamps from plates 1E and 1I also usually show the following characteristics: The design is not strongly recut, the inner lines often are faint, the upper border of the top label block is poorly defined and in about half the copies the upper right diamond block is

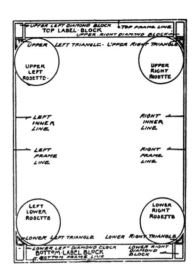

This diagram shows the various components of the 3¢ Washington stamp of 1851-57.

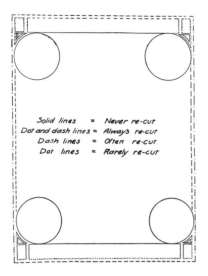

Solid lines = Never re-cut
Dot and dash lines = Always re-cut
Dash lines = Often re-cut
Dot lines = Rarely re-cut

This diagram shows the lines that were or were not recut on the 1851-57 3¢ stamp.

not recut at all. All copies of Scott 10 and 11, the 3¢ imperforate, were recut, as explained and enumerated in the Scott Specialized. As noted, recutting is the strengthening or deepening by hand on the plate of certain lines of the stamp design. Because of the original light impressions on the plate, every stamp had to be recut. The recutting occurred after the impression had been transferred to the plate. This is shown in the adjacent diagram. This and the diagram on page 57 come from the three-volume *The United States Postage Stamps of the 19th Century* by Lester G. Brookman.

Many copies from plate 2E are lightly inked, but all have clear impressions since, in this state, the plate showed no wear. Both plates 2E and 0 show heavily recut inner lines. Also, plate 0 often shows the recut lines broken here and there due to faulty impression. On plate 5E, the recut inner lines are of moderate strength.

Plate 1L occasionally may be found in an orange-brown shade (used as early as October 4, 1851). Plate 1L stamps may show a weak transfer from the transfer roll at the upper right. Impressions often show more than moderate wear because "the plate was used long after wear first appeared, and should have been retired because of worn impressions," according to 3¢ expert Tom Alexander.

Specialist collectors often create chronological color charts of the imperforate 3¢ Washington. Dr. Carroll Chase's work with color was updated by Dr. Wilbur F. Amonette, writing in the May 1973 issue of *The Chronicle of the U.S. Classic Postal Issues.* Chase had classified the colors after studying the stamps used on dated covers. He constructed a master color chart with 210 stamps identified as to color. Dr. Amonette inherited this chart plus several hundred additional stamps identified by Chase as to color. Using the Chase studies, Amonette made changes and additions, and arrived at "a simpler and more complete classification."

As for orange-brown stamps, Dr. Amonette notes that some shades of orange brown are identified only by the plate rather than the color. He says, "All stamps from plates 1E, 1I, 2E, 5E and 0 were produced in what is now considered to be the true orange-brown shade." The other imperforate plates were printed in other colors "except for the rare (but not the true) orange-brown shades of 1852 and 1856."

A greatly simplified rendering of Amonette's color classification of the 3¢ imperforate follows:

1851, orange brown, only color used from July 1 to early October when plate 1L was put into use. Plate 1E produced a rare bright orange brown. The earliest known dates of use of the orange-brown plates, all in 1851, are: plate 1E, July 1; 1I, July 12; 2E, July 23; 5E, July 19; and plate 0, September 8. Fewer than 20 million orange-brown stamps were printed.

1851, experimental orange brown, November, from plate 1L. Slightly different from the true orange brown (October 4), it may be quite bright or dull, but in either case there is very little orange.

1852, brownish carmine, first appeared in November 1851 but predominates in 1852. A bright brownish carmine exists.

1852, orange brown, from plate 2L and 3, probably accidental printings.

1852, claret and deep claret, mostly from plate 1L used early in 1852. A not so deep claret also from plate 1L appeared in December.

1853, dull red. Known to have been used as early as October 1852. During the last six months of 1853, there is an overlapping of the dull red and dull rose. Dull red printings of the second half of 1853 were only fair impressions. A scarce yellowish dull red exists.

1853-54, rose red. Actually produced from March 1853 to early 1855. Known from plate 1L. Most impressions were fair to poor.

1855, orange red. Used mostly in this year, usually poor impressions due to low quality ink. Examples occur from plates 4 and 5L.

1856, yellowish rose red. From late 1855 to July 1856, a wide variety of shades were produced. Striking examples are known from plates 5L and 8.

These 3¢ 1851-57 stamps were applied and canceled in Canada on a letter to the United States.

1856, pinkish. Rare; a variety of the yellowish rose red.

1856, brownish carmine. Mid-1856. Includes plates 2L and 3 as in 1852, but the 1856 brownish carmines show plate wear and poorer impressions.

1856, orange brown. Rare. Unlike the orange browns of 1852, this was an accidental printing.

1857, claret. It appeared in the fall of 1856 but predominantly in 1857. It ranges from grayish or brownish to purplish claret. The grayish and purplish are mostly deep shades.

1857, rose brown, yellow brown. The latter is rarer.

1857, plum. This is the rarest of the 1857 shades. It differs from the deep claret in having more brown.

It should be obvious by now that to specialize in these stamps, one should have a verified color chart. "The commonest error is to identify a common shade as an orange brown," says Amonette. Tips for determining color include using northern daylight if possible, use unused examples or used copies with black cancels (colored cancels can distort the color), and use stamps of good impression without being overinked or underinked. Plate the stamp.

The best examples of the various colors come from the following plates: 1851 orange brown, plate 1E; 1851 copper (orange) brown, 2E only; 1852 brownish carmine, 1L; 1852 claret, 1L; 1853 dull red, 1L, 2L and 3; 1854 rose red, 1L, 2L and 3; 1855 orange red, 2L, 3, 4 and 5L; 1856 yellowish rose red, 4, 5L, 6, 7 and 8; 1856 brownish carmine, 4, 5L, 6, 7 and 8; and 1857, all shades, 2L, 3, 4, 5L, 6, 7 and 8. Dr. Amonette also classifies the colors by rarity, with 8 as the highest order of rarity. The colors he rates as 8 are the 1851 bright orange brown, 1851 yellowish orange brown, 1856 pinkish, 1856 orange brown and 1857 plum.

The Scott Specialized catalog listings for the 3¢ Washingtons are based on colors, printing varieties (notably, types of recutting) and cancellation varieties.

Additional information on plating the 3¢ Washington is available in *Chronicle* 77, 95 and 124. These articles are by William K. McDaniel, another 3¢ specialist. Other worthwhile articles include one in the *American Philatelic Congress Book 1979* and the December 1979 issue of the *American Philatelist*. Each includes diagrams or illustrations of plating varieties. The two essentials for extensive plate reconstruction are a copy of the 1975 revised edition of Dr. Carroll Chase's *The 3¢ Stamp of the United*

States 1851-1857 Issue and a set of photos of the reconstructed plates, available from the philatelic section of the Smithsonian Institution.

The first United States 3¢ Washington imperforate stamps were issued July 1, 1851. They served until early 1857, when the perforated varieties began to appear. The stamps were printed by Toppan, Carpenter, Casilear and Company. They were produced from steel plates bearing engraved designs from a steel die. These plates contained 200 impressions each. The sheets were divided into two panes of 100 stamps each for distribution to post offices.

In *The 3¢ Stamp of the United States 1851-1857 Issue*, Dr. Carroll Chase writes that more than 1.02 billion imperforate and perforated 3¢ Washington stamps were issued between 1851 and sometime in 1861. Of that total, about 362 million were imperforate and 658 million were perforated. The printers used nine plates to print the imperforate stamps. Chase estimated the quantities issued of the orange-brown shade: plate 1E, 2.2678 million; plate 1 intermediate, 4.0502 million; plate 2E, 4.1698 million; plate 0, 4.3618 million; plate 5E, 5.0936 million. Plate 0, made in August 1851, was the fourth one manufactured. It never bore a number; that is why students refer to it as plate "0." It produced only orange-brown stamps.

The paper used for the 3¢ Washington was usually white wove, of rag stock, moderately thick (it averages 3/1,000 of an inch thick) and opaque, high quality and machine made. A few copies are on part-India paper and others on handmade paper. Some production in 1853 may have been on vertically ribbed paper. Gum varies but is mostly pale in color. It ranges from practically colorless to a fairly dark brown. The gum was applied by hand to the panes of 100 after the sheets were printed and cut in half, Chase says.

The 3¢ Washington imperforates were used chiefly to pay the 3¢ per half ounce domestic first-class letter rate. Two of the stamps would pay the one-half to one-ounce double rate or the 6¢ rate for a half-ounce letter going more than 3,000 miles, chiefly coast to coast. This 6¢ transcontinental rate was in effect between July 1, 1851, and April 1, 1855. It helps account for the large number of used pairs of the 3¢ that still survive. To pay the 10¢ coast-to-coast rate in effect from April 1, 1855, to August 1861, it is not uncommon to see three 3¢ Washingtons and a 1¢ Franklin.

The 3¢ Washington imperforate on foreign mail

Two-thirds of a 3¢ 1851 used as a 1¢ on cover to New York. This cover was formerly in the Alfred Caspary collection.

usually is found combined with other stamps to make up a higher rate. Three 3¢ and a 1¢ were sometimes used to pay the 10¢ rate to Canada, Hawaii, Mexico, Panama, Cuba or some of the other West Indian islands. From the Pacific coast to Canada and other British American provinces, the rate was 15¢, and sometimes five 3¢ Washingtons were employed, according to Chase (page 213). Other somewhat uncommon uses were eight 3¢ to pay the 24¢ rate to England, seven to France and, beginning in April 1857, five to France. The rate to Germany as of July 1857 also was 15¢. Occasionally, 3¢ stamps were used on mail from abroad sent to the United States; for example, on letters from Canada prepaid from the border (see photo on page 59), and from Central America and West Indian ports such as St. Thomas. Often this mail was posted aboard U.S. ships.

Bisected copies of the 3¢ 1851 exist genuinely used on cover. These are rare. The 1990 Scott *Specialized* lists under Number 11 a vertical half and a diagonal half used on cover. Bisects never were authorized by law, but postal authorities were inclined to let them pass, prepaying the postage, and did not levy postage due charges. Bisects of the 3¢ generally are found helping to pay two different rates. One is the 10¢ coast-to-coast rate after April 1, 1855, paid by three-and-a-third 3¢ stamps. Or a bisected 3¢ could pay the 1¢ rate on circulars or the 1¢ drop-letter rate in lieu of a 1¢ Franklin. Chase himself owned three examples of the 3¢ bisect helping to pay the 10¢ rate and five others paying a 1¢ rate.

Diagonal bisects are a bit more common than vertical bisects. Chase states that in 20 years of searching, he located only eight to 10 genuine bisects on cover. More recently, Stanley M. Piller, a stamp dealer and collector specializing in this area, has reported the existence of 16 covers showing bisected 3¢ 1851 stamps. Of these, 12 are believed genuine and four "questionable." (See *The Chronicle of the U.S. Classic Postal Issues*, November 1987 and February 1988.]

Brookman, in *The United States Postage Stamps of the 19th Century*, notes "possibly a dozen genuinely used examples" exist. The Philatelic Foundation has certified bisects from Philadelphia; Jackson, Michigan; Jordan, New York; and New York City. Fakes do exist.

Mixed franking covers with the 3¢ 1851-57 and stamps of a foreign country are rare. For example, they are rarer than stamps of the 1869 Pictorial issue used with foreign stamps. The most famous and rarest is the cover shown on this page. It bears a pair of the 3¢ (Scott 11) plus 2¢ and 5¢ Hawaiian Missionary stamps. The stamps pay the 5¢ Hawaiian postage, 2¢ ship fee and the 6¢ U.S. rate to the East Coast from the West Coast. The cover was sent October 4, 1852, and is the only example of the 2¢ Missionary known used on cover.

The 3¢ Washington stamp also is known used on covers with stamps of Great Britain, Victoria and several Roman States.

First day of issue was July 1, 1851. About 30 to 50 first-day covers exist, according to Stanley Piller.

As for large multiples of the 3¢ Washington imperforate, as many as four full panes of 100 stamps are known, either from plate 1L or 3. In his *Census of United States*

This is both the greatest 3¢ 1851-57 cover and the greatest Hawaiian Missionary cover.

Classic Plate Blocks, John Chapin lists two panes with numbers, one from plate 1L (Scott 11). Chase owned an unused block of 39 in orange brown from plate 5E. A block of 12 is believed to be the largest piece on cover, according to Piller. At least three covers are known that are franked with a strip of 10 of the 3¢ imperforate Washington. Ezra Cole recalls seeing a very defective complete used pane many years ago.

The 3¢ Washington is found with a wide variety of cancellations, ranging from black and color killers, year-dated town postmarks, numerals, "PAID," "WAY," "FREE," to carriers, express companies and steamships. The use of stamps to prepay postage was not compulsory on domestic mail until January 1, 1856. During the period July 1, 1851, to January 1, 1856, letters not prepaid were charged 5¢ — as opposed to 3¢ for prepaid. At first, red was the most common cancellation color on the 3¢ orange brown in 1851, but black quickly superseded it as the most common. Chase ranks the cancel colors from the most common to rarest as black, blue, red, green, brown, magenta (actually claret), ultramarine, orange, violet, purple and the rarest of all, olive yellow, used in just two or three towns. Blue was common because it was used in such cities as Philadelphia (1851-53), Cincinnati and Baltimore.

Chase defends pen cancels as perfectly proper and collectible, although the Scott *Specialized* still deducts 38 percent for a pen cancel on the 3¢ orange brown and 43 percent on the 3¢ dull red. As discussed on page 7, pen cancels are found on foreign postage stamps used for revenue purposes, but the United States had no revenue stamps during the 1851-57 period, and no need for them.

Black and blue are the most common colors for town postmarks. Several cities used one color for the postmark and another for the cancel. Boston, for example, used a red postmark and a black killer. Green postmarks are not as scarce as Scott prices indicate. Common true greens include a number of cities; for example, Lancaster, Pennsylvania; New London, Connecticut; Jackson, Mississippi; and Rome, Georgia. Rare colored town postmarks are the claret (sometimes called magenta) of Hartford, Connecticut; the lilac of Winchendon, Massachusetts; and olive yellow, the rarest known, used in Athens, Tennessee, and Littleton, New Hampshire.

Year-dated postmarks from 1851 and 1852 are rare, and from 1853 scarce. New York City used one briefly from July 11 through July 26, 1853. It is scarce.

The 3¢ Washington imperforates are found with a variety of so-called "transportation type" postmarks, including railroads, packet boats, steamships, steamboats and express companies. Private express companies handled much of the mail in the West. But by an act of Congress all mail they carried had to be enclosed in U.S. government stamped envelopes, bearing the same amount of postage they would have had if handled by the government. Prior to 1858, most of the mail from the Pacific coast to the East went via Nicaragua or Panama. Overland, the trip consumed three to five weeks. Butterfield's overland route didn't begin until 1858, and the Pony Express opened in April 1860.

Plate and printing varieties of the 3¢ include shifted transfers, major and minor plate cracks (especially six positions on plate 5L), double and triple transfers, double impressions (at least two examples known), printed on both sides, and the unofficial perf 12 1/2 variety.

Demonetization of the 3¢ Washingtons (imperforate and perforated) began in August 1861 and continued until January 1862. This was to prevent Confederate postmasters from selling remaining stocks of U.S. postage stamps in the North. The Confederate States of America in turn prohibited the use of U.S. postage stamps on and after June 1, 1861. The Confederacy also increased the letter rate from 3¢ to 5¢. Mail sent from the Confederacy after June 1, 1861, was treated in the Union as unpaid matter and held for postage. Such matter was ordered sent to the Dead Letter Office in Washington.

Stamps to be demonetized could be exchanged for the new 1861 issue (Scott 63-65 and 67-72). Stamps from "disloyal" states were not to be honored for exchange. The farther west the state, the later the dates for exchange. Thus it was possible until January 1862 to use the 1851-60 stamps (including the 3¢ imperforate) in California and Oregon.

Sometimes letters with obsolete issues were struck with the rare marking "OLD STAMPS NOT RECOGNIZED." Less often, a "DUE 3 OLD STAMP" marking was applied. A very rare marking on letters from the South, where "Union" postage stamps were not recognized, reads: "SOUTHN LETTER/UNPAID/DUE 3."

By June 1, 1861, 10 states had seceded from the Union. Occasionally, U.S. stamps are seen used to pay postage on letters from the Confederacy after May 31, 1861. That was the virtual end of the use of the 3¢ stamp of 1851-57, except for a handful of illegal late usages.

Chapter 6

1856 5¢ Jefferson

Date of Issue: March 1856
Earliest Known Use: March 24, 1856
Scott Catalog Number: 12
Format: Two panes of 100
Designer: Edward Purcell
Engravers: Joseph Ives Pease (portrait); Cyrus Durand (border); Henry Earle (lettering)
Printer: Toppan, Carpenter, Casilear & Company of Philadelphia
Quantity Issued: 150,000 (estimated)

Just why the U.S. 5¢ Jefferson imperforate stamp of 1856 was issued is not known. We know it is a scarce stamp, one of the scarcest face-different U.S. stamps, often found with skinny margins. It tends to appear with somewhat greater frequency than the 10¢ Washington imperforate recuts (Scott 16), although the two stamps catalog about the same. The 5¢ Jefferson imperforate (Scott 12) has a 1990 Scott retail catalog value of $1,300 used and $10,000 (in italics, signifying infrequent sales) unused.

Students of the 5¢ Jefferson have agonized for decades over why the red-brown imperforate stamp was issued. No one has answered the question with conclusive, documented evidence. However, there are at least three good reasons for its issuance early in 1856. The timing of this release, incidentally, made it the latecomer among the 1851-57 imperforate stamps.

Reasons adduced are:

1. The 5¢ registration fee, established under the Act of March 3, 1855, which became effective on July 1, 1855.

2. The need for a single stamp to pay the 5¢ "inland" rate (shore to ship and vice versa) on mail to destinations abroad, under the U.S.-British postal treaty of 1849.

3. The expected need for 5¢ stamps to make up, or help make up, the 15¢ per 1/4-ounce rate under the U.S.-French postal treaty of March 2, 1857, effective in April 1857.

In addition, a 5¢ stamp would be handy for paying 10¢ rates and multiples thereof, such as various foreign rates as well as the rate to domestic destinations more than 3,000 miles distant. The recently passed Act of

Posted at Albany, New York, in November of 1857, this cover is one of very few on which an 1856 5¢ Jefferson imperf was actually used to pay the 5¢ registration fee. Letter postage was paid by the 3¢ Washington stamp at right.

March 3, 1855, had made prepayment of domestic postage in cash or stamps compulsory as of July 1, and the use of stamps for prepayment of domestic mail was made compulsory as of January 1, 1856.

Stanley B. Ashbrook, the great student of the 1¢ blue Franklin stamps of 1851-57, denied the notion that the stamp had anything to do with registered mail. He wrote: "There was nothing in the law providing for the use of stamps to indicate the payment of registration." Further, he noted: "There was also nothing in the instructions issued to postmasters that permitted them to put a five cent stamp on a letter to show the letter was registered." Ashbrook made much of the fact that the registration charge was referred to as a "fee." For example: "The five cents was always referred to as a 'fee' and naturally the fee was payable in cash."

Premier students Delf Norona and Dr. Carroll Chase tended to agree with Ashbrook. Chase observed that the registry fee was always paid in cash while the 1851-57 stamps were current. But other students differed. One was Philip E. Baker, writing in the May 1972 *Classics Chronicle*: "The motive for the ordering and issuance of this stamp was to pay the registry fee." Baker made note of "bookkeeping problems" that arose from attempts to recoup this compensation. The postmaster was supposed to receive 4¢ of the 5¢ registry fee for handling the letter. Baker said, "Evidently the difficulties in reconciling the accounts between individual postmasters and the [post office] department were insurmountable. Influences were apparently quickly exerted to revert back to the cash payment idea, and instructions were so given."

For more than 30 years, this March 24, 1856, Philadelphia to Nova Scotia cover has stood up as the earliest recorded use of a 5¢ imperforate Jefferson.

In this scenario, one motivation for issuance of the 5¢ Jefferson stamp was quickly altered by the reality of its use. John N. Luff, the dean of U.S. stamp students, stated bluntly in 1902: "The five-cent stamps were for the registration fee." But the preponderance of cash registration payments refutes this.

Elliott Perry, the man who plated the 10¢ 1847, said that the wording of the Act of 1855 "indicated that the prepayment of postage and/or registration was legal by either stamps or cash." In his *Pat Paragraphs*, Perry pointed out that there was no evidence to indicate that the 5¢ Jefferson was not released to pay both regular postage and the registration fee. He also noted that the importance and use of the 5¢ ship-to-shore rate decreased steadily during the 1850s, as there were fewer and fewer destinations to which it applied.

If one wishes to attack either argument further, note two salient facts. First, if the 5¢ Jefferson imperforate was designed for registered mail, why do so few covers survive today showing the stamp paying the fee? Among the very few known are the two covers illustrated in Henry W. Hill's scarce 1955 work, *The United States Five Cent Stamps of 1856-1861*. Both these covers originated at

This block of 11 was for many years the largest surviving multiple of the 5¢ imperforate Jefferson stamp of 1856. The top three stamps were subsequently removed, producing a horizontal block of eight. The block of eight then was broken into two blocks of four. The Walter Klein block of four sold for $27,500 at the September 27, 1988, Christie's auction.

Albany in 1857. One of them, with a 5¢ Jefferson paying the registry fee and a 3¢ imperforate Washington stamp paying the regular letter rate, is shown on page 67. Those who deny the 5¢ stamp was issued to pay the registration fee have to write off these two Albany covers as mistakes.

However, proponents of the registration argument can ask why — if the stamp was issued to prepay the 5¢ inland rate — it wasn't issued until 1856. The "inland" rate had been applicable since before 1850, and the 5¢ 1847 stamp had been demonetized on July 1, 1851. From that day forward, people wishing to pay the 5¢ inland rate by stamps had to resort to using a 3¢ Washington and two 1¢ Franklins.

In summary, official records known to us do not state definite reasons for issuance of the 5¢ imperforate Jefferson in early 1856. Nor do they specifically forbid payment of the registration fee by stamp.

Some philatelic students think the 5¢ Jefferson may have been issued weeks before the earliest known usage, which is a cover mailed March 24, 1856, from Philadelphia to Halifax, Nova Scotia. This cover, illustrated on page 68, has reposed in the Theodore Gore, Mortimer Neinken and Louis Grunin collections. This cover was

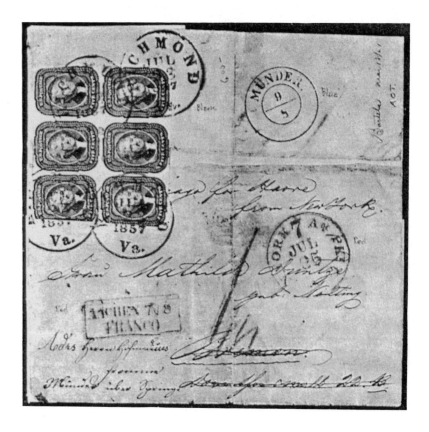

Block of six of the 5¢ imperf, on an 1857 cover from Richmond to Germany.

sold on March 25, 1987, by Christie's of New York for $44,000. The stamp pays the 5¢ shore-to-ship rate to Boston. From there, it went by ship to the maritime province. This cover helps define the period of use of the 5¢ Jefferson imperforates, which ran from early 1856 until about August 1857, when the first 5¢ perforated Jefferson stamps appeared. August 23, 1857, is the earliest known date of use for the 5¢ red brown type I perforated Jefferson stamp, Scott 28.

Lester Brookman estimated that about 150,000 copies of the imperforate Jefferson were issued — the plate having been made late in 1855 or early 1856. John Luff, who made extensive use of statistics when they existed, does not hazard an estimate. He does note that "from 1853 to 1859 the reports of the Postmaster General do not, unfortunately, supply statistics of the quantities of stamps delivered to postmasters or of those sold to the public."

Philip Baker, in the May 1972 *Classics Chronicle*, disagrees with Brookman, saying that more like 250,000 to 300,000 imperforate Jeffersons were issued, and noting that this would supply only about 10 stamps to each post office. But he also notes that the 5¢ Jefferson stamps were used primarily in the "major port cities," such as New Orleans, New York and Boston.

Elliott Perry would probably tend to agree with Brookman's estimate. In his *Pat Paragraphs* he wrote: "In general the smaller offices had 1¢ and 3¢ stamps (or 3¢ envelopes from 1853) by which a 5¢ rate could be prepaid. Probably less than 10 percent of the 20,000 to 28,000 U.S. post offices during the years 1851 to 1860 would have carried a supply of 5¢ stamps for prepaying postage, simply because there was so little need for that value even after the 15¢ rate to France was established."

The 5¢ imperforate Jefferson stamp was printed from one plate only, in sheets of 200 impressions, divided by a center line into two panes of 100 stamps each. A vertical imprint of the engraving and printing firm (Toppan, Carpenter, Casilear & Company of Philadelphia) appears in the left margin of the left pane and in the right margin of the right pane. These imprints appear opposite positions 31, 41, 51 and 61 (left pane) and positions 40, 50, 60 and 70 in the right pane. Stamps from top rows in both panes show position dots outside and to the top of the design. All this was well-known to Earl Oakley when he began investigating how to reconstruct the two panes of the imperforate 5¢ stamps.

Henry Hill had stated in his 1955 book on the stamps: "The chief obstacle was the lack of definite plate marks. It soon became obvious that the plating of the stamp would be most difficult, if not impossible . . . I am not now alone in my belief that the stamp cannot be accurately plated with the present day knowledge, equipment and material available."

Oakley knew that the transfer roll, from which the stamp designs were rocked into the plate, had four different reliefs. By diligent investigation he discovered telltale markings in the colorless oval around the vignette at about the 10 o'clock position. While they don't work for every imperforate Jefferson, Oakley's discoveries were an important breakthrough. His research was published in the July 1963 *Classics Chronicle*.

Large pieces of the 5¢ Jefferson are very rare. The largest multiple known to me was an irregular used block of 11, with pen-mark cancels. This block sold in 1955 for $2,000 at a New York City auction. Since then the top row of three stamps was removed, making a used horizontal block of eight. This has been broken into two blocks of four. The second largest off-cover piece known to me is a used horizontal strip of six, showing margins clear all around. The fifth stamp from left has a preprinting paper fold. This impressive piece was in the Edward Knapp collection. Equally large is the block of six on a cover to Germany used from Richmond, Virginia, in 1857.

In 1963 Frank Levi Jr. of Larchmont, New York, made a survey of surviving multiples of the Jefferson imperfs. Of the horizontal pieces, there were 77 pairs, 31 strips of three, five strips of four, and two strips of six. Of

The "Consul Klep" cover, partially cropped photographically, is called the most famous of all 5¢ 1856 covers. It sold at auction in March 1987 for $121,000. It bears a beautiful strip of three Jefferson imperfs, with full sheet margin at right.

vertical pieces, there were 28 pairs and 20 strips of three. Hill ranked multiples off cover in this order of descending scarcity: blocks, vertical pairs and strips of three, horizontal pairs and strips. On cover, he ranked them: blocks of four or larger, singles, pairs (especially vertical) and strips of three (vertical scarcer).

Levi's investigation showed the most common on-cover usages were: 15¢ to France, 10¢ to California and 30¢ to Germany by Prussian closed mail. Actually, none is common. The 1990 Scott catalog lists a single on cover (to France) at $2,000, a used pair off cover at $2,750, and a used strip of three at $5,000. By 1964, Levi had recorded 188 covers with the 5¢ imperforate Jefferson. Of these, 115 (61 percent) had been sent from New Orleans, 98 of which were destined for France. Approximately 2,500 to 3,000 10¢ 1847 covers exist. I estimate that well under 750 (maybe under 400) 5¢ 1856 covers survive.

Until March 1987, the highest price paid for an imperforate Jefferson cover was $93,500 for the example shown on this page. Dealer Andrew Levitt paid this price at the 1981 Siegel rarity sale. The stamps are: 12¢ imperforate black Washington, horizontal pair; 1¢ blue type II Franklin imperforate; and the 5¢ red brown 1856 Jefferson. The fresh cover shows stamps tied by neat circular red grids, making four-color combination with the adhesives in different colors. This is a 30¢ half-ounce rating to Prussia by closed mail. The rate was in effect from October 1852, to September 1861. A most unusual method of paying 30¢.

The fabulous 1981 realization was eclipsed in March 1987 when the well-known "Consul Klep" marginal strip of three on cover sold for $121,000 at Christie's first sale

The same rate as shown on the cover on page 70, also to Germany, but here in a more unusual franking. The 30¢ postage is paid by two 12¢ imperfs, a 5¢ Jefferson and a 1¢ Franklin (type II).

of the Louis Grunin 1851-57 cover collection. This cover, shown on page 72, was once owned by N. Klep Van Velthoven, consul for Venezuela in Brussels. Consul Klep's collection was sold in 1957 in Switzerland. His 5¢ cover was purchased by Henry Hill, author of the book about the 5¢ imperfs. Lester Brookman called the Klep cover "probably the most famous of all 1856 5¢ covers."

The 5¢ is known used on cover to foreign destinations besides France, but virtually all these are rare: Great Britain, Holland, Spain, Switzerland, Mexico, Sardinia, Italy, Albania, Nova Scotia, Hong Kong and Greece.

The 5¢ 1856 is also known on at least one cover originating abroad. Shown on this page, this cover bears imperforate 1¢, 3¢ and 5¢ stamps (two horizontal pairs) of the 1851-56 issue and originated in New Brunswick. It traveled down to Boston by Colonial Express Mail, and then went via New York City to Glasgow, Scotland. The 24¢ franking pays the rate to Great Britain, with 19¢ credited to England and 5¢ retained by the United States. The red 19 credit marking shows clearly. Uses like this make any cover interesting. When they involve stamps as scarce as the 5¢ imperfs, they are very interesting indeed.

Off cover, the 5¢ 1856 is known with a variety of different cancels, although, of course, not so many as the 1¢ or 3¢ stamps. Colors include black, red, magenta, blue and green. Types are: 1856, 1857 and 1858 year dates; "PAID"; steamship; U.S. Express Mail; express company; steamboat; and railroad.

Two pairs of the 5¢ imperforate, plus a 3¢ and a 1¢, on a cover to Scotland that originated in New Brunswick. This may be the only 5¢ imperf cover that originated abroad.

Chapter 7

1855 10¢ Washington

Date of Issue: early May 1855

Earliest Known Use: Types I and IV: not recorded but likely May-June 1855; type II: May 12, 1855; type III, May 23, 1855

Scott Catalog Numbers: 13 (type I), 14 (type II), 15 (type III), 16 (type IV)

Format: two panes of 100. (Only 20 positions, bottom rows of each pane, are type I; 93 of the 200 plate positions are type II; 79 are type III; and eight are type IV.

Designer: Edward Purcell

Engravers: Joseph Ives Pease (portrait), Henry Earle (border and lettering)

Printer: Toppan, Carpenter, Casilear and Company of Philadelphia

Quantity Issued: 500,000 type I, 2,325,000 type II, 2,000,000 type III, 200,000 type IV (all estimates)

The U.S. 10¢ Washington head stamps of 1855 have much to offer the intermediate collector of moderate means, as well as the advanced collector with substantial resources. These imperforate stamps are found in four basic types (Scott 13-16) that come from 200 positions from a single plate. The two more common types are available as used singles from $100 to $300 each, depending on condition. The two scarcer types cost between $400 to $1,250 each used, for a nice representative single.

After intensive plating research by such students as the late Mortimer Neinken, Frank S. Levi Jr., and Jerome S. Wagshal, positive identification of all the 200 positions has been made, but some are hard to identify owing to weak characteristics. An estimated total of some five million copies of the imperforate 10¢ stamps were issued, and many thousands have survived. Although there seem to be enough around for collectors of 19th-century U.S. stamps — at least of the two commoner types — there is no raging surplus.

The earliest-known use of a 10¢ Washington imperforate is on a cover dated May 12, 1855. The stamp was issued to meet a new rate for letter mail traveling more than 3,000 miles (typically, from the East Coast to California). Effective April 1, 1855, this 10¢ rate replaced the previous 6¢ rate. When the new rate became effective, the United States had no 10¢ stamp. The 10¢ 1847 stamps had been demonetized in July 1851. The new 10¢ green wasn't available until early May of 1855. Distribution was slow. The engravers and printers were rushed, and this shows in the printed product. The design of the stamp, as engraved on the steel die from which impressions were transferred to the printing plate, is not squarely aligned. Thus, the stamp design does not form a perfect

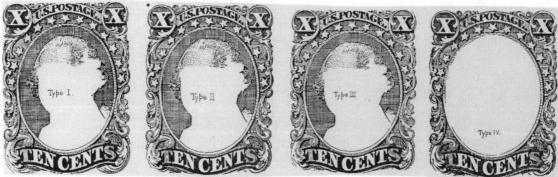

The four different types of the U.S. 10¢ stamp of 1855. The main points of distinction are the completeness of the ornaments at top and bottom. The sketches are from Neinken's book.

rectangle. In his landmark book on this stamp, *The United States Ten Cent Stamps of 1855-1859*, the late Mortimer L. Neinken observed that though the design is "very beautiful," the workmanship is "a bit crude," as if the engraving was done "rather hurriedly."

The four different stamp types result from incomplete transfer of the design from the master die to the 200-subject plate. The plate was too short. The designs of some positions were burnished or short transferred to make them fit. Subsequently, the engravers found that a few positions had been excessively shortened. These were recut by hand, resulting in the scarcest of the four collectible types.

Here follows a description of the four types, along with observations about each:

Type I stamps (Scott 13): These show incomplete design at top. The outer lines above the X's and above the U.S. POSTAGE tablet are mostly missing. However, the bottom design is mostly complete, though the left shell is missing several of its bottom lines. In addition, there's a position dot below the lower left corner. These features are shown in the sketch on the previous page, which is taken from Neinken's extremely useful book. The type I stamps come from the bottom row of the plate. Shown on this page is a fine used type I stamp, with what seems to be a New York ocean mail cancel. Note the wide sheet margin at the bottom, evidence that the stamp came from the bottom row. A position dot might also show at lower left. There are 20 type I positions in the 200-subject plate. Thus, accepting the estimate that five million imperf Washington stamps were printed, 500,000 of them would have been type I. The 1990 Scott catalog lists the stamp on cover at $850, compared with $700 for a used off-cover stamp. In my experience, the on-cover stamp should be valued higher.

Type II stamps (Scott 14): These show incomplete design at bottom. The top of the design, including the outer lines, is complete. There may be a position dot near the upper left corner. At the bottom, the outer line is broken in the middle and both shells are mostly cut away. The type II stamps are the most common of the four types. They come from 93 positions on the plate. Shown here is a very-fine used example, from position 40L (40th stamp on the left pane) showing part of the center line that divided the 200-subject sheet into post office panes of 100 each. The position dot might show, northwest of the X at upper left. Stamps showing part of the center line or,

A type I stamp, showing full shell at lower right and incomplete ornaments at top.

A type II stamp, showing complete ornaments at top, incomplete at bottom.

A type III stamp, showing incomplete ornaments at both top and bottom.

especially, a portion of the left or right plate number and imprint, are obviously more desirable than ordinary copies. The imprint reads: "Toppan. Carpenter. Casilear & Co. BANK NOTE ENGRAVERS. Phila. New York. Boston & Cincinnati."

Type III (Scott 15): These show incomplete design both top and bottom. At the top, the lines are missing above the top label and above the X tablets. The shells at the bottom are also cut away, especially at the right, where there are no shell lines below the S in CENTS. A large portion of the bottom line below TEN CENTS is missing. Type III stamps come from 79 positions on the sheet, 39 from the left pane and 40 from the right. A large-margined used copy with a black grid cancel is shown in the accompanying photo. Note how much of the design is missing both top and bottom. The type III stamps, with an estimated two million issued, are modestly less common than type II, with 2,325,000 issued.

Type IV (Scott 16): These are the stamps that were re-engraved by hand after the designs had been transferred to the printing plate. Only eight positions of the 200 on the plate were re-engraved, so the resulting stamps are elusive. The recutting consists of enhancements in the outer framelines above POSTAGE and below CENTS. The recutting was mostly done on the left pane. Four positions were recut at top (65L, 74L, 86L and 3R); three were recut at bottom (54L, 55L and 76L); just one, position 64L, was recut at both top and bottom. Note that positions 54-55L and 64-65L form a block of four stamps — all type IV, showing the three varieties of recutting. At

A lovely pair of the 10¢ Washington, showing type IV (at left) and type II. Though it may not show well in this photo, the line above POSTAGE in the type IV stamp has been re-engraved.

least one such block has survived, according to Neinken. Shown on the opposite page is a lovely used pair of 10¢ imperfs, on which the left stamp is a type IV, showing recutting at top. The right stamp is type II. The pair comes from positions 74L and 75L.

Only about 200,000 type IV stamps ever existed — four percent of the total five million 10¢ imperfs estimated to have been printed. These stamps are scarce, so it should come as no surprise that some clever fakes have been created from the more common types, by forgers who carefully draw in recut lines. Detection is possible because each position in the 200-subject plate has its distinguishing characteristics, and fakes are always made from incorrect positions.

Plating of the U.S. 10¢ green Washington imperforate stamps — using stamps to reconstruct the configuration of the original sheet — has been greatly helped by the survival of a large number of pairs and strips, as well as larger multiples. Shown is a used vertical strip of three, from plate positions 76R, 86R and 96R. The top stamp is a type II, the middle stamp a type III and the bottom stamp is type I. So here we have three different Scott numbers (14, 15 and 13) se-tenant in a single strip.

The largest surviving multiples of this stamp, both mint and used, are in the much-honored collection of Ryohei Ishikawa of Tokyo. The mint item is a horizontal strip of eight from positions 71L-78L. Two of the stamps are type IV, the rest type II. The used piece, which is the largest known multiple of the 10¢ imperforate Washington stamp, is a vertical block of 21 (three by seven) from positions 1-3L through 61-63L. This block consists of 10 type II stamps and 11 type III stamps.

The second largest known multiple is a square block of 16, formerly in the Arthur Hind collection, which was sold in the 1930s. This remarkable block, from positions 42-45L through 72-75L, contains five different examples of the scarce type IV recut stamps, showing all three varieties of recutting.

The third largest known multiple is a horizontal block of 12 (six by two), from the right pane of the 200-subject sheet, positions 42-47R and 52-57R. This block was in the Alfred Caspary collection, auctioned in 1956. It most recently appeared in the late John Kaufmann's Gems sale in December 1985, where it realized $13,750.

The 10¢ Washington imperforate stamps are generally found in three basic colors: green, dark green and yellowish green. The stamps are most often found on

A vertical strip of three U.S. 1855 10¢ Washington imperforates, showing types II, III and I. Here we have three major U.S. Scott numbers (14, 15 and 13) in one strip.

A U.S. 1855 10¢ imperforate Washington stamp, type IV (Scott 16), on a government envelope (with Wells Fargo imprint) sent from California to Philadelphia.

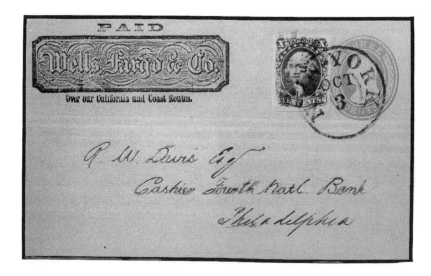

domestic covers paying the 10¢ transcontinental rate (for distances over 3,000 miles) or on covers to Europe, chiefly to France and less often to Germany. Covers to England from this era usually bear the 12¢ Washington, Scott 17. The 10¢ Washington imperforates were used mainly in 1855-57, but are known from 1858-59 and (rarely) later.

Cancellation varieties are not so varied as on the 1¢ or 3¢ imperforate stamps. Cancellations found on all four types of the 10¢ stamp include year date, paid, steamship, territorial, express company, numeral and manuscript. Stamps with pen cancels bring prices about half those commanded by stamps with handstamped postmarks. At least six different cancellation colors are known: black, blue, red brown, ultramarine, magenta and green, in approximately that order of scarcity. On the underlying green stamp, red and magenta cancels are the most striking. Some cancellation varieties, such as territorial and express company markings, are associated with the development of mail services in the Old West.

Shown is a 10¢ imperforate, type IV (position 55L, recut at bottom) on a 3¢ embossed envelope (Scott U10) addressed to Philadelphia. At the left on this envelope is the imprint of Wells, Fargo & Company, with the text "Paid over our California and coast routes." For an unstated but substantial fee, Wells Fargo carried this cover from California (possibly Sacramento) to New York. As the postmark indicates, the cover actually entered the U.S. mails at New York City. To comply with the law, such privately carried mails had to be contained in government entire envelopes. The coast-to-coast U.S. postage rate was 10¢, and this had to be paid, even though the sender didn't use the government mails. With the cover, the sender apparently found it easier to overpay postage than to apply the required 7¢ in stamps to the 3¢ envelope.

A rarer and more spectacular use is shown below. Here a 10¢ type II stamp, tied by the New York ocean mail cancel, pays the U.S. postage from the East Coast to San Francisco. The envelope is a printed California Penny Post Company entire (Scott 34LU13A) showing 5¢ prepaid for private local delivery in California. In addition, the cover bears (at right) a blue 1¢ Swarts local adhesive (Scott 136L14), which prepaid private carriage to the post office in New York. This combination of mail services, one government and two private, makes the cover extremely unusual and a great rarity. The cover is also very well-preserved, the only fault being that the 10¢ stamp is slightly cut into at right. This cover sold for $38,500 as part of the Louis Grunin collection, auctioned by Christie's (New York) in March 1987.

Western covers with the 10¢ imperforate are sometimes illustrated with mining scenes, which are highly sought after. More rarely, one finds postal-history-related scenes, such as that on the cover on page 82. Here the wood engraving shows a group of San Franciscans waiting outside the post office, while a noisy carrier announces the arrival of the Panama steamer with the latest news from the east. The stamp on the cover is a type II, pen canceled. The manuscript postmark indicates an 1856 use from Clarksville, California, to Vermont. This cover sold for $2,310 in the same sale as the California Penny Post cover.

While casual observers might think that the imperforate Washington stamps have been studied to the point

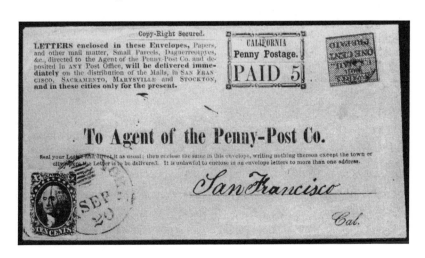

A 10¢ imperforate, type II, used with a blue New York Swarts local adhesive on a printed entire envelope of the California Penny Post Company.

Another type II stamp, here pen canceled on an 1856 cover from Clarksville, California, to Vermont. The wood-engraved cachet shows a crowd at the San Francisco post office, while in the foreground a noisy carrier announces the arrival of the steamer from Panama with the latest news from home.

where nothing more is to be learned, that's far from the case. Much more work remains to be done on these stamps. Some areas offering research possibilities:

1. Nailing down the remaining unplated positions for plate 2, used to print some of the perforated stamps, of which a number of plating positions are still in doubt.

2. A study of the 10¢ imperforates used on covers handled by the express companies.

3. Studies and censuses of 10¢ imperforate stamps used in the West Indian mails and on covers sent to the Orient. There is much more to be learned.

Chapter 8

1851 12¢ Washington

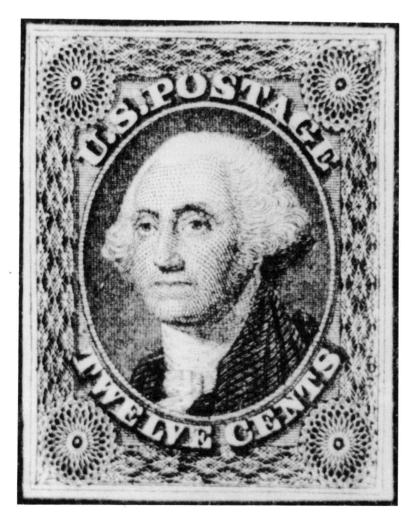

Date of Issue: July 1, 1851
Earliest Known Use: August 4, 1851
Scott Catalog Number: 17
Format: two panes of 100
Designer: Edward Purcell
Engravers: Joseph Ives Pease (portrait), Cyrus Durand (border), Henry Earle (lettering)
Printer: Toppan, Carpenter, Casilear and Company of Philadelphia
Quantity Issued: 2,500,000 (estimated)

A margin copy of the 12¢ 1851 from position 51L, showing part of the printer's imprint.

The 12¢ black imperforate Washington stamp of 1851 is a stamp that was never really needed. Off cover, pairs are almost as common as singles. On cover, bisects are more common than single uses! A strange stamp indeed. But a desirable one.

As recently as December 1988, a collector was willing to pay $3,575 for an incredible used single, more than 14 times catalog. The same buyer bought another used copy at the same auction for $578. And at about that time, an unused block of four brought well under $3,000 — against an $11,000 Scott catalog value.

Ostensibly, the 12¢ imperforate Washington was issued on July 1, 1851, the same date as the 1¢ blue Franklin and the 3¢ orange-brown Washington stamp, which have been discussed in previous chapters. Between 1851 and mid-1857, an estimated 2,468,800 copies of the 12¢ imperforate stamp were issued. This compares with about 3.7 million 5¢ Franklins of the 1847 series. During the first four years of the 12¢ imperforates, only about 870,000 copies were issued. After mid-1855, when prepayment of domestic postage by stamps had become mandatory, production increased.

The 12¢ Washington shows a three-quarter face portrait of our first president, after a portrait by Gilbert Stuart, surrounded by a tessellated frame with lathework rosettes in the four corners. "U.S. POSTAGE" surmounts the portrait oval, with "TWELVE CENTS" beneath. The vertical stamp design measures 20 millimeters by 25mm. The stamp was printed in various shades of black: gray black, black, deep smudgy black and intense black.

The imperforate 12¢ stamps were all printed from a single plate of 200 subjects, divided into two square panes of 100 stamps each. The stamps were printed very close together, which helps account for the scarcity of four-margin copies and for the high prices paid for jumbo copies showing portions of the adjoining stamps. In the sheet margins, right and left, was the imprint of the engraving and printing company: "TOPPAN, CARPENTER, CASILEAR & Co. BANK NOTE ENGRAVERS, Phila., New York, Boston & Cincinnati."

While specialists refer to it as plate number 1, there was no number on the plate from which the imperforate 12¢ stamps were printed. The designation "plate 1" is needed because an additional plate exists, plate 3, which was used in the late 1850s to produce the perforated versions of this stamp. The plating positions for the 12¢

imperforate stamp have been elaborately reconstructed. Specialists would say that the unnumbered "plate 1" has been plated. All 200 positions can be identified. For example, position 51L1 refers to position 51, the first stamp in the sixth row (a left margin copy) of the left pane of plate 1. If the left margin is big enough, a portion of the imprint will show, as illustrated on the opposite page on a stamp from position 51L1.

Despite the intense study of this stamp, done by such students as Lieutenant Colonel J.K. Tracy, Stanley Ashbrook, Earl Oakley, Mortimer Neinken and others, new information continues to surface. Neinken wrote: "Despite exhaustive studies and research published on the U.S. stamps, especially the earlier ones, more information continually becomes available . . . the end never seems in sight. Thus no research work, no matter how great, can be considered to be the last word."

The 12¢ 1851 stamp is no exception. The only work in the last 60 years that even remotely can be called definitive on the 12¢ 1851 is Neinken's handbook, which was published by the Collectors Club of New York in 1964. The book is mostly a plating study, and it contains just 74 pages. The bulk of it is devoted to large diagrams showing the minute (but unique) identifying characteristics of each of the 200 plate positions. These characteristics consisted mostly of recutting done on the outer and inner lines of the rectangular frame that surrounds the stamp. Engravers performed this recutting right in the plate, before any stamps were printed. The framelines around the design thus show strengthening in various locations, which serves to identify the stamp's position on the plate.

Why were the outer lines, and often the inner lines, recut? Apparently, the original framelines were not en-

Corner margin block of 10 of the 12¢, from the right pane.

Reverse side of a 12¢ 1851 "printed on both sides" variety.

graved deeply enough into the master die. They transferred lightly, or with skips, when the design was transferred from the die to the plate. The lines then had to be strengthened, recut in places on the plate, before the plate was turned over to the printer. Imagine trying to piece together this plate puzzle by using various margin copies and multiple pieces, as Ashbrook and Neinken did. Such feats of plating were one of the great accomplishments of an earlier generation of philatelists.

Margin copies with imprints, such as the 51L1 stamp shown on page 84, are rare. About 20 are known. Imprints are found in the margins alongside positions 40, 50, 60 and 70 on the right pane, and alongside positions 31, 41, 51 and 61 on the left. No complete panes of the 12¢ 1851 stamp survive. The largest mint piece is thought to be a block of 30, 10 by 3, with sheet margin at the top, in the Ryohei Ishikawa collection. An unused block of 12, 4 by 3, was in the William H. Crocker collection. There is also an upper left sheet corner block of 10, from the Henry Gibson collection, and a square block of nine, formerly in the Alfred Caspary collection. The Edgar Jessup collection contained a block of 18, 9 by 2, used on a large legal envelope to a San Francisco law firm. This is the largest used block reported, on or off cover.

One of the largest used blocks known to me is a square block of 16, canceled by black grids and red crayon, also in the Ishikawa collection. Two used blocks of eight are known, both with Philadelphia cancels. There is a horizontal strip of 10, somewhat defective, showing blue Nashville cancels. This was in a recent Kelleher sale.

There are a number of printing varieties on the 12¢ Washington stamp, including copies printed on both sides. Perhaps four examples are known of this rare variety. Triple transfers occur in positions 5R and 49R. Position 49R is most unusual, showing pronounced shifting in the lower right, in "TWELVE CENTS" and in the lower right rosette. The most pronounced double transfer is found at position 27R. This stamp shows a doubling of every letter in the top label ("U.S. POSTAGE"). All four rosettes also show doubling.

The normal paper on which the 12¢ Washington stamp is found is hard, white wove, ranging from very thin to thick. A few copies are known on a thin, part-India paper that is distinctive.

The stamp can be found with a fairly wide variety of cancellations. The most common are black grid, blue town and red grid. The 12¢ is also found with brown, magenta, orange and green strikes, all of which are scarce to rare. Other cancels include paid, way, steamship, steamboat, supplementary mail, railroad and manuscript. Pen cancels lower the value about 50 percent. Two quite rare cancels are "Honolulu" in a red circular datestamp and "U.S. Express mail."

I previously stated that the 12¢ imperforate Washington stamp of 1851 was never really needed. This is reflected in several odd facts about the stamp. Off cover, pairs are almost as common as singles. And on cover, bisects are more common than single uses. The *Scott Specialized Catalogue of United States Stamps* says, "The 12¢ was for quadruple the ordinary rate." This may have been the intent, but the 12¢ stamp was seldom used for this purpose. If a 12¢ stamp was created for quadruple-rate uses, why was no 6¢ stamp issued for vastly more common double rates? In fact, the United States didn't issue a 6¢ stamp until 1869. (A 6¢ stamped envelope appeared in June 1863.) In May 1958, the Robert A. Siegel auction firm of New York City sold the famous Emmerson Krug collection of classic United States covers. The Krug collection contained 26 12¢ imperforate Washington covers. One of these is illustrated here. This 1857 cover from Brooklyn bears a pair of 12¢ Washingtons, paying the 24¢ transatlantic rate to England. In England, a perforated 1-penny Great Britain stamp was added, right on top of the pair, to forward the cover from London to Derbyshire. The result is a very attractive mixed franking.

Only seven of the 26 12¢ Krug covers were domestic

A pair of 12¢ imperforate Washington stamps on cover from Brooklyn to London in 1857, forwarded with the addition of a British 1-penny stamp, completely covering one stamp.

uses. And only three of these showed the stamp paying the 12¢ quadruple domestic rate. These three represent about 25 percent of the known examples. Such uses are scarce. One domestic cover bore a bisected stamp, and the remaining three were overpayments of the 10¢ coast-to-coast rate (over 3,000 miles) effective April 1, 1855. Nineteen of the 12¢ Krug covers went abroad, mostly to England. Of these, 16 were franked with pairs of the 12¢. The other three each bore four copies, being double 24¢ rates to England or Ireland.

If so many pairs were needed to pay the 24¢ rate to the British Isles, why did the post office wait until 1860 to issue a 24¢ stamp (Scott 37)? For that matter, why wait until 1860 to issue a 30¢ stamp for multi-rate uses to France, Germany and elsewhere? We'll probably never know the answer. Economy was certainly a factor. Back then, the post office wanted to issue as few stamps as possible.

As the Krug holding suggests, the most common use of this stamp was on 24¢ rate covers to the British Isles. That's why off-cover pairs are almost as common as singles. And as the Krug holding also suggests, on-cover singles are scarce.

There were only three possible justifications for the lone use of a 12¢ stamp. One is for the four-times domestic rate under 3,000 miles. As we have established, such uses are scarce. The second possibility is on a double-rate cover to or from the Pacific Coast during the 6¢-for-over-3,000-miles period, July 1, 1851, through March 31, 1855. (At that time, the rate increased to 10¢ single, 20¢ double.) The third possibility is for a single 12¢ stamp paying the 10¢ single rate from the Pacific

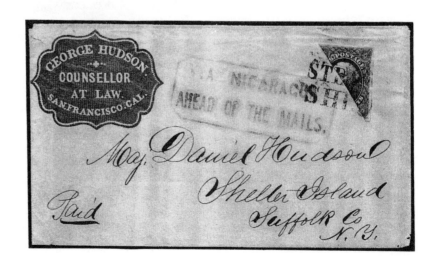

Bisected 12¢ imperf Washington, well tied, on a "via Nicaragua" cover from San Francisco to New York. This cover dates from the fall of 1853, when the San Francisco post office had run out of 3¢ stamps.

Quadrisected 12¢ imperforate, on a 3¢ entire envelope from Canton, Mississippi. The quartered 12¢ Washington stamp is tied by pen marks with an accompanying notation "1/4 of 12¢." This cover was declared genuine by Stanley Ashbrook, but it has never received a Philatelic Foundation certificate.

Coast, beginning April 1, 1855, until demonetization in 1861, plus a 2¢ ship fee. Realistically, this means covers from Hawaii, although other possibilities exist.

Additional information will be found in the November 1973 issue of *The Chronicle of U.S. Classic Postal Issues*, in an article by Thomas J. Alexander titled "The Single 12¢ Stamp of the 1851-1861 Issue on Cover." Some 63 single on-cover uses of the 12¢ imperforate stamp have been recorded. The majority of these are 10¢ plus 2¢ covers from Honolulu.

Another *Chronicle* article (August 1972) lists some 100 bisect uses of the 12¢ stamp. This is the only U.S. stamp, perhaps the only stamp in the world, for which the bisected use is more common than the use of a whole single stamp. The bisect covers are relatively numerous for a reason. During the last half of 1853, the San Francisco post office ran out of 3¢ stamps and possibly 1¢ stamps as well. Rather than just take cash, the postmaster elected to bisect 12¢ stamps to pay the 6¢ coast-to-coast rate. A number of covers from San Francisco to the East Coast bore 12¢ bisects. The cover shown on the opposite page is extra interesting because of the embossed lawyer's corner cachet and the "via Nicaragua" handstamp. The two-line "STEAM/SHIP" marking nicely ties the bisected portion of the stamp, which is a prerequisite for collectibility.

Some eastern postal officials accepted these bisect uses; others did not. To eliminate confusion, the Post Office Department issued a circular on November 10, 1853, that said in part, "... neither does the law authorize the use of parts of postage stamps in prepayment of postage." Bisect covers from before the date of this

89

circular are much more acceptable to philatelists than those after it.

Bisected 12¢ stamps were also used to pay the double and triple 3¢ domestic rate. A rare use is as a 6¢ stamp, along with 3¢ and 1¢ stamps, paying the 10¢ rate to Canada. Equally rare is a bisect paying part of the 29¢ rate from the West Coast to England. Diagonal bisects are by far the most common. Vertical halves are much rarer. Several quadrisects — one-fourth of the 12¢ stamp — have been reported. The one shown on page 89 from Canton, Mississippi, was examined by Stanley Ashbrook in 1956 and found to be "genuine in every respect." Lester Brookman reports other examples as having been found and carelessly destroyed. However, I don't believe any quadrisected 12¢ 1851 cover has ever received a genuine opinion from the Philatelic Foundation.

In addition to the bisects, there is a small number of unusual and noteworthy 12¢ imperforate covers. Shown is a cover on which three 10¢ imperforate type 3 stamps and a 12¢ imperforate pay the 42¢ rate to Sweden via the Prussian closed mails in 1857. A stunning cover with a pair of 12¢ stamps plus 1¢ and 5¢ imperforates, paying the 30¢ rate to Glogau, Prussia (now Poland), has sold twice in recent years for more than $90,000.

More can be said about the 12¢ Washington imperforates. Just why the stamp was issued bears further investigation. A collection of covers to foreign destinations other than England would be breathtaking. Updated censuses of single uses on cover, and bisect uses, is overdue. Even more useful would be a census of all known covers.

Three 10¢ imperforates along with a 12¢ make the 42¢ Prussian Closed Mail rate on this 1857 cover to Sweden.

Conclusion

Early in 1857 the imperforate stamps of the United States gave way to perforated issues of similar designs. These new stamps, of perf gauge 15-15 1/2, made stamp separation much easier and, some believed, improved adhesion to envelopes. Franklin, Washington and Jefferson are portrayed on the perforated issues of 1857-61, just as on the 1847-56 imperforates, making collecting the first perforated issues a logical extension of an imperforate collection.

The 1847 issue, the 5¢ Franklin and 10¢ Washington, had both been declared invalid to pay postage as of July 1, 1851. Beginning in August 1861, the Post Office Department began invalidating the 1851-56 imperforate and 1857-61 perforated stamps. This was done in part to prevent usage of stamp stocks in former U.S. post offices now located in the Confederate States.

Whereas domestic letter postage rates gradually dropped, first to 3¢, then in 1883 to 2¢, rates on mail sent abroad continued to be high for some time until the uniform rate system under the Universal Postal Union began in 1875. To satisfy postage requirements on the increasingly higher volume of high-cost foreign-bound mail, three new values were added to the 1857-61 perforated issues: 24¢ (Washington), 30¢ (Franklin) and 90¢ (Washington again).

Although today at least there are probably enough 5¢ and 10¢ 1847 covers to go around, there are relatively few remaining that were mailed to foreign countries, Canadian provinces being the commonest destinations. As this is written, the market for 1847s is weak, and 1990 may be a good time to begin a collection of these handsome stamps.

All of the rarer types of the 1¢ Franklin, and copies

of the 5¢ imperforate Jefferson, especially choice copies and those on cover, are in short supply. Large-margined copies of the 12¢ black Washington imperforate are also desirable. Many shades and usages, as well as some plate positions of the 3¢ imperforate Washington, are rare and in demand too.

We are fortunate, I suppose, that Americans of the late 1840s and the 1850s carefully separated by knife or scissors many of the imperforate issues, providing us with the four-margin copies we so prize today. In fact, today's market demands four-margined, sound copies. Those of lesser quality bring big discounts from catalog or other standard value.

Note also that many of the early perforated issues, in fact most of them, come with poor to average centering as a rule. The first perforation machine used in the United States, a $600 modified rouletting device from William Bemrose & Sons of Derby, England, was in use subject to the imprecisions and mistakes of the operator. There was little room on the sheets for stamp margins outside the designs anyway. The printer, Toppan, Carpenter & Company, delivered the first perforated stamps, the 3¢ type I Washingtons, to the government on February 24, 1857.

As noted in the text of the foregoing book, there are still many facets of the U.S. 1847-56 imperforates ripe for philatelic study. Plating, shades, earliest usages, as well as rates, routes and markings of covers, come to mind immediately. New finds continue to be made, although not so often as in the past.

When one considers covers with classic stamps, virtually each one of which is unique in several ways, today's prices seem a bit less daunting. This uniqueness and philatelic antiquity enhances pride of ownership.

There is a plethora of information available about these classic imperforates for a beginner, and my hope is that this book gives a jump start to your endeavors. If you are already familiar with these stamps, this book should serve as an up-to-date summary reference work.

Index